T0031429

Cyndi Dale is an internationally renowned author, speaker, and healer. She has written more than thirty books, including *Llewellyn's Complete Book of Chakras*; *Energy Healing for Trauma, Stress, and Chronic Illness*; *Kundalini*; and *The Complete Book of Chakra Healing*. Her year-long apprenticeship program through her company, Essential Energy, assists individuals in developing their natural intuitive and healing gifts. She also teaches in-depth classes via the Shift Network. Visit her at CyndiDale.com.

SACRAL CHAKRA

YOUR SECOND ENERGY CENTER
SIMPLIFIED + APPLIED

EDITED BY
CYNDI DALE

Llewellyn Publications
WOODBURY, MINNESOTA

FIRST EDITION
First Printing, 2023

Book design by Rebecca Zins
Cover design by Cassie Willett
Illustrations on pages 16 and 104 by Llewellyn Art Department

Llewellyn is a registered trademark of Llewellyn Worldwide Ltd.

Library of Congress Cataloging-In-Publication Data

Names: Dale, Cyndi, editor.
Title: Sacral chakra : your second energy center simplified and applied / edited by Cyndi Dale.
Description: First edition. | Woodbury, Minnesota : Llewellyn Publications, [2023] | Summary: "As the second book in Llewellyn's Chakra Essentials series, Cyndi Dale provides everything you need to know about this sensual energy center in part 1. In part 2, energy experts—including Anthony J. W. Benson, Nitin Bhatnagar, Jo-Anne Brown, Amanda Huggins, Margaret Ann Lembo, Gina Nicole, Tia Tuenge, Amelia Vogler, and Susan Weis-Bohlen—teach you about this chakra's color associations, intuitive style, physical reach, psychological influence, and more. Connect with this wheel of energy for a more balanced and fulfilling life through dozens of hands-on practices, including yoga poses, visualizations, mantras, essential oils, crystals, and affirmations, as well as recipes specific to your sacral chakra"—Provided by publisher.
Identifiers: LCCN 2023020361 (print) | LCCN 2023020362 (ebook) | ISBN 9780738773315 (paperback) | ISBN 9780738773391 (ebook)
Subjects: LCSH: Chakras. | Energy medicine.
Classification: LCC BF1442.C53 S23 2023 (print) | LCC BF1442.C53 (ebook) | DDC 131—dc23/eng/20230707
LC record available at https://lccn.loc.gov/2023020361
LC ebook record available at https://lccn.loc.gov/2023020362

Llewellyn Publications
A Division of Llewellyn Worldwide Ltd.
2143 Wooddale Drive
Woodbury, MN 55125-2989
www.llewellyn.com
Printed in the United States of America

CONTENTS

List of Practices...xi

Introduction...1

PART 1: ESTABLISHING THE FOUNDATION OF YOUR SECOND CHAKRA KNOWLEDGE [9]

1: Fundamentals...11

2: The Physical Side...35

3: Of the Psyche and the Soul...43

PART 2: APPLYING SECOND CHAKRA KNOWLEDGE IN REAL LIFE [59]

4: Spirit Allies...63

MARGARET ANN LEMBO

5: Yoga Poses...79

AMANDA HUGGINS

6: Body Wisdom...93

NITIN BHATNAGAR, DO

7: Self-Healing and Grounding…107

AMELIA VOGLER

8: Guided Meditations…121

AMANDA HUGGINS

9: Vibrational Remedies…133

JO-ANNE BROWN

10: Crystals, Minerals, and Stones…149

MARGARET ANN LEMBO

11: Mantra Healing…161

TIA TUENGE

12: Colors and Shapes…173

GINA NICOLE

13: Recipes…187

Part 1: ANTHONY J. W. BENSON, 188
Part 2: SUSAN WEIS-BOHLEN, 195

Conclusion…203

PRACTICES

Making a *Vam* of It…19

Be Blue…24

Left Nostril Breathing to Activate Water and Moon…25

Meditating on Your Svadhisthana…32

Try On Your Second Chakra Archetypes…50

Emotional Empathy: Is It Your Own
Feeling or Someone Else's?…53

Activating the Second Chakra in Yoga…84

Full Yoga Sequence to Activate Your Second
Chakra…86

Opening Your Sacrum…102

A Svadhisthana Mudra…104

Establishing Safety for Emotional Healing…110

Balancing Your Second Chakra and Auric Field…111

The Lotus Petal Meditation for Clearing
the Sacral Chakra…113

Resourcing with an Ally…116

Color-Based Visualization for Sacral Healing...124

The Witnessing and Honoring Meditation...126

Pleasure and Creativity Activation: A Moving
Meditation...129

Receive a Second Chakra Attribute Through Sacred
Geometry...144

Use Remedies to Find Balance in Your
Relationships...145

Releasing Sacral Cords by Visualizing Etheric
Gemstones...156

Formulating a Mantra, Step 1: Inner Exploration...165

Formulating a Mantra, Step 2: Making a Yes Map...166

Formulating a Mantra, Step 3: Turning Yeses into
Mantras...166

Drawing on Tradition by Chanting *Vam*...169

Activate Water Using a Shape...179

Using a Circle to Release Tension...180

INTRODUCTION

Please join me in a visualization.

You are standing in a forest at midnight. You are near a lake. Its waters are calm, serene, tranquil, and as smooth as glass. The moon shines brightly overhead. Peering into the water, you see the moon shining there too.

The resulting feeling? It's the same as the feeling that is constantly available through a balanced second chakra. In keeping with our visualization, I like to call it the water-moon chakra because it enables the flow of emotions, intuition, and creativity while reflecting the beauty of the soul.

Located in the abdominal area, your second chakra is called *svadhisthana* in Sanskrit, the best-known source of chakra information. It is also commonly called the sacral chakra due to its location. This subtle energy center, a common vessel for self-growth in yoga, is the topic of this book. It is also the second in an eight-book series called Llewellyn's Chakra Essentials.

This amazing, bite-size series began at the beginning: that is, with a book focused on your first chakra, called the *muladhara* or root chakra. That cherry-red ball of flame lies underneath the cheerful orange chakra that we'll be focusing on in this book. Each additional book beyond this one will add another color to your chakra palette, all the way to the eighth book, which features five out-of-body or extraordinary chakras. (More on those special chakras later!) Does it matter what order you enjoy these books in? Not at all. Each stands alone.

Right now it's time to learn all things awesome about svadhisthana. Your second chakra is like a scented flower. When well-adjusted, it supports you in embracing your sensuality, including all the smells, sights, sounds, and sensations of the somatic (bodily) experience. It also introduces you to feelings. The moon symbolizes emotions and intuition, which often ride together. With expertise in the emotional, your sacral/water-moon chakra actualizes your deeper desires and needs while serving as the basis for compassion and empathy.

Our feelings also prompt creativity. What's your joy? Do you like to paint, write, dance, cook, sing, or indulge in fashion or interior design? Even accounting can be creative if done the right way. Whenever you are breathing your soul into the world and sensing its response, you're engaging the magical universe of your second chakra.

We can thank the ancient Hindus for the term *chakra*. In Sanskrit, the lovely and archaic language of the Indus

Valley, the word means "spinning wheel of light." The yoga paradigm stairsteps up the seven chakras anchored in the spine, each of which manages a specific set of functions, to reach the penultimate goal of enlightenment. Enlightenment—"being in the light"—is a combination of self-realization and unity with all. The truth is that this concept isn't only an ancient Hindu one. Many cultures, including the traditional Hopi, Mayan, Aztec, Berber, and African Kemetic, based their spiritual medicine upon knowledge of chakra-like centers and corresponding, albeit invisible, structures.

What is the importance of embracing every chakra? Humans have long understood that we are composed of energy. Chakras are the brains behind our ability to access and use energy, defined as information that moves. There are two types of energy, however, and that distinction explains the importance of learning about—and interacting with—your chakras.

Physical energy makes up the normal world, and of course you want to be able to comprehend how you function physically. However, more than 99.999 percent of any object, including your body, is made of subtle energy[1]—the

---

1 Ali Sundermier, "99.9999999% of Your Body Is Empty Space," Sciencealert, September 23, 2016, https://www.sciencealert.com/99-9999999-of-your-body-is-empty-space.

stuff that organizes physical energies. The job of managing your subtle energy lies in your chakras, which are considered a subtle energy system or structure.

Your chakras are also the chief rulers of the other two subtle structures: subtle channels and fields. Altogether, your subtle centers, channels, and fields compose your subtle energy anatomy. Right from the get-go, I'm going to give you a cheat sheet about these non-chakra structures because you'll interface with them in this book.

The two main types of subtle channels are the meridians and the nadis. Meridians flow through the connective tissue and carry subtle energies throughout the body. While the term originates in traditional Chinese medicine, these energy pathways are described in subtle ideologies around the world. The term *nadis* is Hindu in origin and chiefly equates with your nerves. Many of the body's thousands of nadis interact directly with the seven in-body chakras.

Every chakra also generates its own field of energy, called an auric field or layer. Together they form the twelve-layer auric field. Each layer encircles the body and serves as a protective barrier, energetically selecting which energies can enter or exit based on the programming in its correlated chakra. Here we'll be focusing on the second auric field since it's the outer layer of your second chakra.

If you are wondering why I teach a twelve-chakra and auric field system, I do so for several reasons. First, because I perceived twelve chakras around living beings when I was a child. Of course, I didn't know those orbs of light and sound were called chakras. I was Lutheran, and the idea didn't exactly come up in church. On top of that, I was raised for several years in the Deep South—not a lot of chakra talk there either. But the twelve balls of energy were obvious to my physical eyes. As an adult, I worked with shamans around the world while studying energetics both spiritually and scientifically. I discovered that the "norm" of working with a seven-chakra system, the typical model used in the West, isn't all that normal. Systems around the world have described anywhere from three to dozens of chakras.

Since my first book came out decades ago, my twelve-chakra system has become internationally renowned. Those extra five chakras are popular as they greatly expand your ability to become the miraculous and powerful being you are. You'll learn about the five extraordinary chakras in the eighth book in this series.

Now let me share the adventure in the pages ahead. Part 1 is written entirely by me. Within these three chapters are the nuts and bolts you'll need to understand in order to become an expert on your own sacral chakra. Most of this data comes from the traditional Hindu bed of knowledge, and some of it is more up to date. At times I'll insert practices so you can make this material your own.

The first chapter covers various details I list for all the books in the series, including the chakra's overarching purpose, location, names, color, and sound. I'll also relay the associated elements, breaths, lotus petals, and even the affiliated god and goddess.

In chapter 2 I'll examine the physical nature of your second chakra. Every chakra is linked with a region of the vertebrae as well as an endocrine gland and other parts of the body. I'll clue you in to the physical systems run by your second chakra, as well as the disease processes that can impact an imbalanced second chakra. I'll complete the first part of the book in chapter 3 by adventuring into the psychological and spiritual functions of your second chakra. What fun to open the jack-in-the-box of joy that is this awesome energy center!

Part 2 is all about life improvement. To get you going, I'll discuss intention and then walk you through a meditation to activate your second chakra. After that, it's all about relating to your sacral/water-moon chakra.

Each chapter of part 2 is written by a subtle energy expert. First, you'll meet your spiritual allies. Once introduced to them, you'll then plunge into poses—yoga ones, that is. Next, you'll learn all about body-based activities that will create a resilient and healthy second chakra.

Second-chakra meditations will help you create balance before you jump for even more joy. And you'll find that chakra balancing is easy and gratifying when achieved via specific vibrational remedies, stones, sounds, shapes, and colors.

Let's get real—and happy! How can you attain a healthy self, including a vibrant sacral chakra, without good food? Our final chapter will leave you salivating as it's chock-full of recipes to stoke your second chakra. Satiate yourself by dining on the recipes offered by our vegan and Ayurvedic chefs, with suggestions from the latter about how to add meat protein.

Now it's time to return to the opening of this introduction. You are standing near the water, looking deeply into a mirroring of the moon and your own sacral chakra.

Let us begin with reflections about the second chakra and its foundational components.

PART 1

ESTABLISHING THE FOUNDATION
OF YOUR SECOND CHAKRA KNOWLEDGE

• • • • • •

Place a hand on your abdomen. Breathe deeply. As you picture this area of your body being bright orange, you also acknowledge whatever emotion is predominant in your body right now. Go ahead—imagine a different shade of orange. Go lighter or deeper. Does your feeling change just a little?

You have just connected with your second chakra, also called your sacral chakra, the subtle energy center that manages your feelings, basic senses, and creativity. I call it the water-moon chakra because of its sensitivity to empathy and compassion. It ensures not only that you *know* who you are but can also *express* who you are.

In this part of the book, I'm going to lay a foundation of knowledge so you can understand the important components of your second chakra. In the first chapter, you'll mainly learn from the rich resources inherited from the Hindu cultures, with a few dabs of modern realizations thrown in. Chapter 2 will enhance your comprehension of the physical nature of your sacral chakra, and chapter 3 will flesh out the psychological and spiritual wellspring that relates to this chakra. A few practices sprinkled throughout will get you acquainted with this beautiful, reflective pool of what is ultimately the energy of love.

1

FUNDAMENTALS

What would life be without taste, touch, and your other senses—without access to your deeper emotions or even the surface ones that ripple quietly, never leaving a mark?

Your second chakra initiates you into the different textures of life, from sensations to emotions. It's also charged with an amazing alchemical process. Within the cauldron of your sacral chakra, sensuality and emotionality blend to formulate creativity.

Because of this chakra, you can lavishly enjoy your individuality while bonding with others. You can drink from the waters of life, nourish yourself on the nectar of joy, and let go in wild abandon. You can *be*.

In the Hindu tradition svadhistana reflects the element of water. I personally attach the representation of the moon to this chakra as well. In many cultures the moon reflects our dreams. There are light and dark sides to the moon, dreams seen and unseen. As you learn about the fundamental components of the second chakra in this chapter, I encourage you to keep these two ideas in mind. The liquid quality of life and the nature of your desires come together through this, your sacral/water-moon chakra.

I'll begin this chapter with a real-life example of how this chakra operates and then describe more detailed aspects of this chakra. Much of this essential information stems from Hindu traditions and has been developed over thousands of years in various Eastern cultures. You'll also be introduced to a practice that will leave you feeling refreshed, as if you've just dived into a clear, crystalline lake under the moon.

THE ESSENCE OF YOUR SECOND CHAKRA

John had prostate problems. These impact millions of men every year and can range from infections to cancer. The prostate is a part of the second chakra, as are other areas of the body you'll learn all about in the next chapter.

I'm an energy healer, not a doctor. I picture subtle energy, however, as interconnecting the physical and spiritual aspects of the self. The frequencies that the second chakra comprises largely deal with emotions. That knowledge clued me in on how to approach John's challenge.

I asked him to tell me about any heavy-duty emotional traumas or situations he had experienced in his life. One stood out immediately. When he was young, he had been mocked by a group of kids from his neighborhood. One boy had even punched him in the abdomen. What was their issue? John, whose given name was really Juan, was Hispanic. His was the only family of color in a white area.

I helped John sense into the various repressed feelings still locked in his second chakra area. He also worked with a therapist to reframe the beliefs he'd unconsciously acquired from that horrifying experience. He figured out that his sticking point, which had previously prevented him from diving into the trauma, had been a feeling of shame. To cope with the bullying, he decided he had to hide his heritage. After graduating from college, he put on a suit and called himself John.

Eventually John figured out that the bullies were acting out their parents' fears. Why did he need to reject his own family roots, he reasoned, because of their insufficient understanding? John switched his name back to Juan and began to embrace the strength and courage of his Hispanic roots. There was a lot to be proud of. His father and mother had entered the United States as immigrants and built up a strong business, which enabled them to bring some of their relatives to their new home country.

Once he dealt with the deeper pain lying in his sacral chakra, Juan emerged more whole. He began to celebrate his family's traditions with them, even letting his mother teach him recipes her own mother had shared with her. He began to eat healthier and get more exercise, two life activities that often get thrown to the wayside when we feel shame. And he summoned the bravery to undergo an experimental medical procedure that cleared up his prostate issue.

As Juan's storyline depicts, your second chakra is vital to your existence and your ability to thrive. It processes your feelings, which are a significant part of your identity. In turn, your emotions inform you about the world and how best to express yourself in it. When blocked, that second chakra can influence your physical and, obviously, your psychological health. When balanced, that basin of emotional truth allows you to show your spiritual essence in the world; joy follows.

Now that you've been shown a bit about its power, you'll love learning more about all aspects of the second chakra throughout part 1.

Overarching Purpose

As your second chakra, svadhisthana rules your emotions, creativity, and sensuality.

IT'S ALL IN THE NAME:
TERMS FOR THE SECOND CHAKRA

The Sanskrit name for the second chakra is svadhisthana. *Sva* means "self" and *adhisthana* means "dwelling place, seat, or residence." Add these parts of the word together and you arrive at the overall meaning of the term: "the abode of self." This means that when you embrace your second chakra, finding a soft nest within it, you nourish your true self.

Additional names include several found in the Tantras: *adhishthan*, *bhima*, *shatpatra*, *skaddala padma*, and *wari* chakra. The later Upanishads added the word *medhra*. Still another name for this chakra is *shaddala*.

LOCATION OF THE SECOND CHAKRA

This chakra lies a mere three centimeters above *muladhara*, the Sanskrit name for the first chakra. For perspective, your first chakra, which governs physical survival and security, is anchored in your coccyx. Your second chakra is between the coccyx and the sacrum and two inches or so under the navel.

If you want to be even more specific, your sacral/water-moon chakra is related to the upper border of your sacrum, including the triangular bone in the spinal column wedged between your two hip bones. This site is about halfway

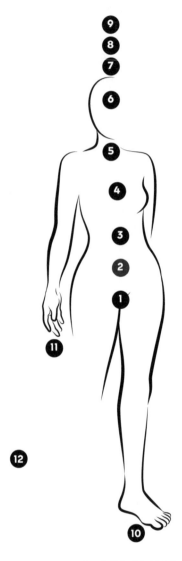

FIGURE 1: THE TWELVE-CHARKA SYSTEM

between the navel and sex organs and nine inches above the seam of the perineum.

As detailed as the last description is, there are different ideas about the exact location of this chakra. Depending on the source, your svadhisthana is said to occupy various regions of the genitalia, abdomen, sacrum, or navel (although the latter is usually ascribed to the third chakra). The most agreed-upon answer is that its nerve plexus lies in the pelvic region, although the voting seems equal on whether it's linked to the sacral, hypogastric, or prostatic nerve plexus within that area.

Because all accounts link the second chakra to the sacrum, it is often called the sacral chakra. You can see your second chakra on figure 1, the twelve-chakra system. Note that the twelfth chakra is an energetic field that surrounds the body.

COLOR OF THE SECOND CHAKRA

Each chakra operates along a different set of frequencies. This band of energy can be distinguished by a particular range of colors and sounds. I'll talk about the sound of your second chakra in the next section.

As for coloration, your sacral chakra serves the subtle energies in the orange spectrum. Right below it lies your first chakra, which operates in the red zone. Above it is your third chakra, which manages yellow energies. Orange is a delightful mix of red and yellow. That point shows you how interactive the chakras are with each other. They buzz along as their own independent units but also interact with the chakras near them. You'll learn ways to employ colors to clear and clean your second chakra in chapter 12.

Orange is known as the cheeriest of all colors. It adds to the hues of sunrises and sunsets, the perfect reflection of its ultimate role of representing your emerging consciousness. While the first chakra establishes your fundamental survival, your second chakra invites the expansiveness of your individuality. Orange also symbolizes emotional activity and positive spiritual qualities such as compassion, faith, and joy.

SOUND OF THE SECOND CHAKRA

There are many terms used to label the tone held within every chakra. They are called *bijas* (seed sounds), as well as *bija mantras* (master sounds). Specifically, a mantra is a sound that encourages a meditative state. Every chakra is associated with a specific bija, or seed sound, which you're encouraged to chant or muse upon to bring about the desired change.

These days the second chakra has become related to the D note. It is part of a sequence of tones that begins with a C in the first chakra and ascends accordingly.

Historically, however, the Hindus have assigned the sound *Vam* (pronounced "vum") to this beautiful chakra when it is being chanted. *Vam* is the sound form of Varun, a derivative of Varuna, god of the oceans and creation. Whenever you focus on *Vam*, you bring into yourself the soothing, feminine sound of the waves against the sand.

Chapter 11 is devoted to interacting with sound while working with your sacral chakra.

PRACTICE

MAKING A *VAM* OF IT

Want to know how to utilize *Vam* to enhance your second chakra? Shape your lips in a circle and push air through them, as if into a tube, to vocalize this sound as "vum." At the same time, picture your sacral chakra. This bija mantra will increase the flow of life energy through your second chakra and remove any insecurities associated with it.

Sound Carrier

A special being is considered the carrier of the second chakra sound: the crocodile (*makara*), which represents sexual vigor and your sensual nature. The crocodile is representative of Varuna, the lord of the sky, ocean, and waters, who uses the waters and the Milky Way as his medium.

Reflect on the nature of the crocodile. It can change from being lethargic to violent in a flash. Inherent in the second chakra are all the ways of the crocodile, from the laziness of sunbathing to the trickery required to surprise its prey.

Connecting to the crocodile energy inside your second chakra presents you with a critical choice. You can be either emotionally available or deceptive, based on your desire.

LOTUS PETALS AND APPEARANCE

Lotus petals are a famous depiction for all in-body chakras. Each individual chakra has a different number and color of petals.

At one level, the petals describe the swirling motion of a chakra. Chakras absorb, process, and release the subtle energies related to their band of frequencies. Chakras interact with physical energy too. Because of this, they are affected by the movements of the physical organs, fluids, sound waves, and electromagnetic frequency (EMF) activity in their localized area. Now, how do the lotus petals fit in? If you were to freeze the spiraling energies of a chakra, you would see a vortex with several outstretching arms of EMF. Those arms would look like the petals of a lotus flower.

There is another level to lotus portraiture. As a flower, it is deeply revered in Hindu society as a symbol of a spiritual life. Lotuses are rooted in muddy water, yet their blossoms reach toward the sun, clear of the murky water. Water itself is considered the *maya* (illusion) of life, and the petals are representative of our true selves.

There are six petals in the second chakra, each of which links to a different nadi. As I covered in the introduction, nadis are subtle energy channels that relate to the nerves. These petals are vermilion with a touch of carmine and represent the six *vrittis* (mental modifications), which are thoughtforms we must shift in order to mature: indulgence, the absence of empathy, destructiveness, delusion, disdain, and suspicion. The letters on these petals are expressed as bam, bham, mam, yam, lam, and ram.

SECOND CHAKRA SYMBOLS:
THE YANTRAS

A *yantra* is a geometric diagram. Yantras have been used for over 13,000 years in Indian culture as assists in meditation. Most yantras, or symbols, represent specific gods and goddesses. It is thought that when the devotee focuses on the yantra symbol, they might receive healing and insight from its related deity. Yantras can also serve to remind us of a specific task or vow.

The yantra of the sacral chakra contains a silver crescent, symbolizing the moon, within a white circle, epitomizing water. The combination of these signs signifies the relationship between water and the moon, a theme I've already proposed in this book.

The moon has many connection points to the second chakra, including the fact that all living beings cycle through many chemical and emotional fluctuations during the moon's transformative phases. As well, because it is associated with the genitals, svadhisthana relates to procreation; in women there is a strong connection between the menstrual cycle and the moon.

In this yantra we find Brahma as the "golden womb" or "cosmic egg" from which all knowledge is born, as well as Rakini, who is described later in this chapter.

GROSS ELEMENT

According to East Indian religions, matter is composed of four basic elements: earth, water, fire, and wind (or air). Many systems also endorse a fifth element, which is space. The element of the second chakra is water.

The water or *jala* element has many facets: it flows, freezes, evaporates, and more. It moves on the ground but can also float in the sky as a cloud before it rains down upon us. Always, however, water is what it is, no matter how many times it changes shape.

Your water-moon chakra is similar in that it is made of one substance that can transform with great fluidity.

Color of the Gross Element

In Hinduism the gross or major element of this chakra is water. Envision the colors of water: transparent, white, or light blue. It is thought that the Creator gave as much blue as possible to nature to ensure that there was enough of this majestic energy to fill the ocean, rivers, and sky.

Any god or goddess that is blue, such as Krishna, is a channel for the powerful qualities of blue, which include courage, stability, fortitude, and determination. When you pull from the blue energy within your second chakra, you are accessing these same strengths.

BE BLUE

The qualities provided through blue, the main color of the second chakra's gross element, center on bravery and fortitude. Are you involved in a situation that requires these types of supportive virtues?

If so, take a couple of deep breaths. Focus on the circumstance and place a hand on your abdomen, the home of your second chakra. Imagine that this energy center is replete with oceans of blue light. What shades, hues, and intensities are available to you?

Next, focus again on the situation at play and imagine that every component is awash with the array of blues available to you. As well, every time you breathe in, you inhale blue. When you exhale, the blue carries out whatever you're ready to release.

Now that you are as blue as Krishna, let go of the process when you're ready and bravely step forward.

LEFT NOSTRIL BREATHING TO ACTIVATE WATER AND MOON

How can you most fully activate your relationship with the water related to your second chakra?

Water is intimately tied to the moon, as we see in the influence of the lunar cycle on the sea's tides. We also know how the moon's phases influence our body chemistry as well as emotions, and they link us to the stars.

We automatically evoke lunar energy when the water element is dominant in the nasal cycle, which is reflective of the regular energetic oscillations of two specific nadis.

The sushumna is the main nadi of the body. It equates to the spine. There are two other vital nadis: the ida and pingala. These climb from your first chakra and move up the body, crisscrossing each other at your chakras. The ida is most often linked to your parasympathetic nervous system, which helps you relax. It is considered a lunar or feminine nadi. The pingala is associated with your sympathetic nervous system, which makes you excited. It is related to solar or masculine energy.

For sixteen minutes every hour, we breathe primarily through our left nostril, which activates our ida or lunar nadi. The ida nadi also stimulates the right side of our brain, which relates to intuition, emotion, and creativity.

Sometimes we want to intentionally practice left nostril breathing, which will enhance the water and moon qualities of our second chakra. To do this, I recommend an approach used in swara yoga, which features the science of nasal breath, among other techniques.

The nose is of particular importance in achieving chakra and physical balancing because it is linked through the olfactory lobe to the hypothalamus, the part of the limbic system (fight, flight, fawn, or freeze) that controls emotions and motivations. The hypothalamus is of particular importance in second chakra or emotional matters.

By breathing solely through the left nostril, you enhance your ability to benefit from the many life activities linked to the second chakra, such as playing music, gardening, doing volunteer work, serving others, showing up compassionately, parenting, and offering friendship.

To perform left nostril breathing, simply sit in a comfortable position and block your right nostril with one or two fingers, then inhale through your left nostril. Breathe in through the left and exhale through the right while blocking the left nostril for one to three minutes.

NOTE: Avoid this exercise if you have high blood pressure or heart disease.

PREDOMINANT SENSE
AND SENSORY ORGAN

All too often we think of chakras as only subtle or ethereal. However, chakras are located within—and help run—the body proper. As an example, each chakra manages a specific sense and the organ that relates to it. The sense associated with svadhisthana is taste, and the sense organ is the tongue.

Taste is a major sense. How often do we make decisions about the foods we want to eat or avoid based on how they taste, which is noticed through our tongue? Many of us can even evoke a taste by simply imagining a food.

Do you need proof? What happens in your mouth when you picture a lemon?

You'd be well served to make decisions about foods and beverages based on your like or dislike of their taste. Our body naturally selects the nourishment it needs based on taste preferences.

ACTION ORGAN

All chakras are associated with an action organ. This is the part of the body that invites physical energy into that chakra and keeps it thriving. For your second chakra, the action organ is your genitals: the testes and the ovaries. This relationship between the sacral chakra and your genitals furthers the sense that it enhances your sensual desires and enjoyment. You'll learn more about these genitalia, which serve as the chakra's major endocrine glands, in the next chapter.

VITAL BREATH

In Hinduism the most vital life force is called *prana*. This is the mystical energy that moves through all living beings, providing movement, animation, and our very existence. It is also called spirit breath, breath of life, and the vital principle. Prana permeates all of reality and is considered a subtle energy. The dense or obvious manifestation of prana is the breath.

There are five different types of prana, which are also called *vayus* (winds). The second chakra is associated with one of these vital breaths, the *apana*. In relation to the second chakra, apana is associated with movement, change, and intense emotions. It balances the flow of physical fluids, emotions, and intuitive messages coming into and exiting this chakra.

ATTRIBUTE

An attribute is a quality. Every chakra is bestowed with a specific and special quality that is related to its sound carrier. In the case of the second chakra, as I already shared, your sound carrier is the crocodile. The ultimate gift of the crocodile is purity. If you fail to integrate this attribute into your experience, you can be prone to attachment or perversion. Paradoxically, crocodiles are frightening and can serve the bondage of materialism, but when we work through our attachments, we are left pure and free.

RULING GODDESSES

The most often cited goddess related to your sacral chakra is Rakini, or Chakini Shakti. She is a two-headed, four-armed goddess who sits on a red lotus and holds an arrow, skull, drum, and ax. She is one of the many forms of Kundalini Shakti. Her two heads represent the split energy of the second chakra: the difference between "I" and "other." Rakini is the inspiration for art and music.

An alternative goddess associated with svadhisthana is Sarasvati, who holds two simultaneous roles with Brahma as the creator of knowledge: she is both his daughter and his wife. It is Sarasvati who forms his consciousness into knowledge.

RULING GODS

The most common god assigned second chakra status is Brahma, the "One God," in his form as the consciousness or golden womb. As such, he is the creator of knowledge.

An alternative depiction is Vishnu as the presiding deity. Vishnu is the lord of preservation and sits on Garuda, the king of birds, who represents the five *vayus,* or breaths. His presence indicates the need to manage the release of kundalini through the breath.

RULING PLANET

The planet ruling the second chakra is Pluto, for its transformational qualities. As of late, Pluto has lost its status as a full-on planet, but it still represents regeneration and rebirth.

RELATED AURIC FIELD

The auric field for the sacral chakra is the second auric layer. In the twelve-chakra system, the second auric field is found about four to five inches away from the skin. It is right outside the tenth auric field, following the first auric field, which lies within the skin and outward to about an inch and a half around the entire body.

This field is programmed by the second chakra and includes our ancestral experiences and beliefs, influences from our family of origin, childhood and adult events, cultural and societal norms, and the events that relate to our emotions, pleasures, and intimacy. These programs are the software that determines which subtle energies that match our second chakra enter or exit our system. Do you want to attract different types of people? Be more empathic or less empathic? Alter the programs in your second chakra. Many of the exercises provided in part 2 will help you do this.

BENEATH YOUR SECOND CHAKRA

Below your second chakra is your first chakra. There is an entire book in this series devoted to your muladhara, or root chakra, which is the base of your existence. Within that chakra, your kundalini—a special type of divine energy—lies coiled, awaiting her climb. Her first stop will be your second chakra, which she will activate to bring awareness to your emotions and bodily senses.

While your first chakra is devoted to the development of your core identity—the place where you get to say *I am*—your second chakra adds movement. In other words, you express *I am being*. What a wonderful shift to move from knowing the self to showing the self.

MEDITATING ON YOUR SVADHISTHANA

This practice will clear your second chakra so you can receive its benefits. Begin with any form of meditation you prefer, from gentle breathing to taking a calming walk. Then let yourself concentrate on these points:

» Imagine the moon reflecting off water. Saturate yourself with the feminine and psychic energies of the moon and the cooling rhythm of the waters. Feel the fluids in your own body finding their right flow and function as the Vishnu powers in your soul bring restoration to you, linking you to the Milky Way above for the perspective of spiritual truths. The crocodile watches, and you see in him your ego-based qualities—from lethargy to violence—as well as your ability to lie in wait before attacking your goals.

» Next, absorb the vermilion or orange-red of the six lotus petals and repeat the bija mantra *Vam* (pronounced "vum"), sensing the corresponding nadis in your body opening to healing. Challenges such as lust, anger, greed, and jealousy gradually transform into opportunities for compassion, peace, and understanding. The crocodile begins to smile; his basic nature now understood, he offers redemption and transformation.

» Watch as Brahma opens the cosmic door of consciousness and presents Rakini. Like a mirror, her ax reflects all that is not spiritual before it cleaves all lies from your soul. Her drum beats with a mantra that restores your natural rhythm, while her spear sets you free from such lotus petal vices as disdain and delusion. Finally, she holds her skull to your face. You stare into the eyes and see your romantic nature—along with her final gift, the release from the fear of death. Your crocodile nature has now been smoothed into that of a spiritual warrior, one who wages kindness toward love.

You have now furthered your own personal charisma, as well as your ability to serve as the beloved of Brahma, holding on to the truth of your life rather than the stories of it.

SUMMARY

As you've learned, your sacral chakra is your emotional base. The second chakra receives the kundalini from the first chakra to activate your emotional and sensual powers and needs, providing you the depth of empathy, intimacy, and compassion. Because of your water-moon chakra, you understand the beauty of sensuality as well as the importance of regulating your desires.

Colored orange, the main tone of this chakra is *Vam*. It is carried by the crocodile and helps you relate to the sense of taste, which is noticed via your tongue. The action organ through which this chakra expresses is your genitals.

Symbolized by a silver crescent moon, this watery chakra shines with the white or light blue of the water element and assists you with gaining purity and releasing attachments. With six petals on its lotus, it is also affiliated with the goddess Rakini and the god Brahma, as well as the planet of Pluto.

Now that you've considered the fundamentals of your second chakra, it's time to delve into the physicality of this watery, moonlit chakra.

2

THE PHYSICAL SIDE

Though most of reality consists of subtle energy, your second chakra is an incredibly important determinant of your physical health. Essentially, your sacral chakra's overriding physical job is to manage the systems within its region of the body.

As you read all about this physiological energy center, prepare to enrich your understanding of both your sacral chakra and your own dynamic health.

OVERVIEW OF THE SECOND CHAKRA'S PHYSICAL REACH

Your second chakra is in your lower abdomen—both front and back sides. Associated with your sacrum, it's an environment rich in physicality.

Housed in the sacral vertebrae, this chakra's physical impact stretches throughout the entirety of your abdominal area. Imperative functions are performed by its major endocrine glands, the gonads, with the key associated endocrine glands being the testes in men and the ovaries in women. The reach of your sacral chakra's functions also includes other organs and body areas associated with the reproductive and digestion systems, among others.

But that's not all. As you'll learn in the next section, there is an extremely important "brain" in your second chakra, and it manages just about everything about you, from vulnerability to disease to emotional balance.

As you can already gather, there is a reason the second chakra has been considered such a critical component of both your chakra zodiac and life.

AREAS OF THE BODY MANAGED

Your second chakra manages many life activities, including those related to your sexual organs. In biological women, these include the uterus, vagina, ovaries, and cervix. In biological men, the specific organs include the testes, penis, and prostate. (During the rest of this book, any references to men and women refer to the biological sense, not how one identifies.) This chakra also manages the pelvis in general, the lower vertebrae, the appendix, parts of the upper and lower intestines, and aspects of the kidneys, bladder, and digestive organs.

Critical to understanding the second chakra's range is to know that it essentially includes your enteric nervous system, also called the gut brain. Its connection to the enteric system is probably the most powerful part of your second chakra.

There are many parts of the body that help process emotions, including your head brain and your physical heart. But neither of these centers of intelligence compares to your gut brain, which plays a gargantuan role in composing your feelings and emotional reactions as well as impacting your overall physical health.

Basically, your gut brain, which is situated smack-dab in the middle of your sacral chakra, is your digestive system's processing center. It contains networks of neurons that are buried in the walls of your digestive tract and run from your anus to your esophagus. This secondary brain manages your digestion as well as your response to stress. It also makes neurotransmitters that connect it to your central nervous system.

Some of the most exciting news recently regarding the body is an approach to emotional and physical health that focuses on the vagus nerve. This nerve passes from your head all the way down through your torso. It holds your social programming, meaning the codes that determine your responses to stress. At least 90 percent of the signals that run along your vagus nerve pass from your sacral chakra's gut brain to your head brain, not the other way around.

Hats off to the ancients. Thousands of years ago, they were clear that the sacral chakra composes your feelings. Science is proving that they were correct, and more so. That vagus nerve also carries messages from the gut brain to your head's decision-making center regarding your digestion, state of immunity, and more.

We now know that at least 100 million bacteria live in the gastrointestinal tract (think second chakra), along with fungi, parasites, and viruses. You usually live symbiotically with these microbes, which form a microbiome in your enteric nervous system. When all is well, these microbes assist with metabolic functions and fat distribution, and they can even prevent you from getting sick. But if the gut is off, such as happens if you're eating poorly, taking antibiotics, undergoing severe stress, or harboring resentments, your vagus nerve conveys a negative set of messages to your brain. Anything might happen then, from anxiety and depression to illness.

As ample research has shown, it pays to pay attention to your sacral chakra.

ASSOCIATED GLAND:
YOUR GONADS

As I've already shared, the main endocrine glands for the sacral chakra differ in men and women, but they are basically your gonads or sexual glands.

The main second chakra endocrine gland in men are the testes or testicles. These two oval-shaped reproductive glands produce sperm and testosterone. They lie behind the penis in a pouch of skin called the scrotum.

The prostate gland is shaped like a doughnut and weighs about an ounce. It is located just below the bladder, behind the pubic bone and in front of the rectum. It wraps around the urethra, which carries urine from the bladder to the penis. Its primary job is to help control the flow of urine, and it also assists with creating semen. Most typically we find the prostate associated with both the first and second chakras in men and fed by the energy of both. It can become damaged or dysfunctional if a man resists the first chakra's life forces or the second chakra's ability to embrace the fullness of emotion and expression. Any distorted beliefs about sexuality, pleasure, or emotion can show up as a problem in the prostate.

The ovaries are the woman's core second chakra endocrine gland. They are a pair of glands, each about the size and shape of an almond, in the female reproductive system.

They primarily make estrogen and progesterone and store the eggs that will drop into the uterus for fertilization via the fallopian tubes. After menopause, the ovaries stop producing these hormones but continue making testosterone and androstenedione, which provide critical protection against heart disease.

What occurs if you have healthy gonads, as well as a healthy relationship between them and the entirety of your second chakra? In men, the testes can produce an appropriate amount of testosterone, which enables support of the adrenal hormones. For both men and women, the gonads create emotional stability and help magnify the personality. We can therefore help prevent the inflexibility, stiffening, and sexual repression that can come with age.

It is interesting that the adrenals—which are the main endocrine gland for your first chakra—and the testes and ovaries all relate to the kidney meridian line in traditional Chinese medicine. This meridian and the kidney organs themselves are especially vulnerable to excessive stress and sexual abuse, conditions that gravely affect the first and second chakras. I point this out so that you know how delicate our lives are—and how vital are both the first and second chakras.

RELATED PHYSICAL STRESSORS, PROBLEMS, AND ILLNESSES

Problems with the second chakra often result in health issues involving the reproductive, digestive, and urinary systems, as well as the enteric nervous system. Specific issues might arise with immune challenges, menstruation, sexual dysfunctions, prostate issues, chronic lower back pain, sciatica, joint problems, loss of sensual pleasure, appendicitis, all "itis" diseases of the bowels (such as diverticulitis), and compulsions including carbohydrate addictions.

As you know, the second chakra is anchored in the sacral vertebrae. That implies that any issues with those vertebrae as well as the pelvis are intertwined with second chakra concerns.

SUMMARY

Your sacral chakra has been known as the source of emotions and pleasures for nearly forever. Knowing about the physical organs and systems related to this chakra proves the accuracy of this statement.

This chakra's vibrant role in your physiology begins with its anchoring site in the sacral vertebrae. Within this region of the body are pleasure organs, including the main endocrine glands of the sacral chakra: the testes for men and ovaries for women. Yes, these gonads are about reproduction, but they are also about physical stimulation and joy.

Many of the organs and systems associated with reproduction and digestion are also found within this basin of your body, including your enteric nervous system. Also called your gut brain, herein is your microbiome, the neurological and digestive processes that determine not only much of your immune response but also your emotions. Bottom line: if you want a healthy body, go for the gusto with your second chakra–related choices.

Want to know even more splendid information about your sacral chakra? Keep on moving. Let's discuss your psyche— the nature of your psychology and your soul.

3

OF THE PSYCHE AND THE SOUL

In many cultures the word for "psyche" and "soul" is the same. In this chapter we'll be simultaneously examining the second chakra's connection to your psychological health and to your soul or spiritual nature.

What are the various psychological and spiritual facets of your water-moon chakra? There might not be a more dynamic question to ask. As we'll cover, your second chakra is the most powerful determinant of your emotional and mental well-being. All aspects of your feelings are involved in your sacral chakra, as is your approach to sensuality and the pleasures of the body.

Through this chapter's exploration, you'll learn about the various facets of psyche involved with this chakra, as well as when it first goes online, or becomes active. I'll also clue you in to the various messages provided by your sacral chakra's feelings and offer practices to make this data real.

How about the archetypes associated with this chakra and the various intuitive gifts available through it? All this information and more will add zest to your understanding of your second chakra's functionality, bolstering your ability to make effective decisions about everything from intimacy to relating empathically.

And in the conclusion, in the same way that the moon reflects infinity in the waters of life, you will be invited to become the reflection of your best self in the world.

OVERARCHING PSYCHOLOGICAL IMPACT

Svadhisthana initiates and sustains bonds when we are in relationships. It also serves as a primary chakra defining the types of relationships we attract.

Most of these connections are emotional in nature; as such, they can be healthy or unhealthy, gratifying or empty. Basically, this chakra links emotional reaction with emotional attachment.

Within the context of this chakra, we access our sensual nature and therefore our identity relating to the sex/es or gender/s we are attracted to. Fantasies and moods can create intense fluctuations as we struggle with desires and the attraction to pleasure.

This chakra can sway us into shortchanging ourselves or indulging in abusive behavior toward others, especially emotionally. Maybe we too often indulge in envy, jealousy, rage, or greed. If this is the case, we might want to face the beliefs we have acquired that cause prejudice, resentment, and complex fears. Perhaps we overreact emotionally to certain situations—or maybe even underreact. If we swing one way or another, we are being asked to illuminate our inner shadows and become disciplined enough to create patterns of self-vigilance. We do this by accessing and employing three fundamental types of shakti, which are extensions of the kundalini energy that is provided us through our first chakra.

- » **PRANA SHAKTI:** vital force
- » **DHARANA SHAKTI:** the power of concentration
- » **CHETANA SHAKTI:** the power of consciousness

Ultimately we must accept the belief that we are lovable in relationship to others and can trust our emotions to help us steer the way.

I have experienced the emotional power of the second chakra in my client work many, many times. Utmost in my mind is work I did with a man who hadn't maintained a romantic relationship with a woman for longer than two years—and he was fifty years of age. I asked him to describe his relationship with his mother, the mother being our primary template for Shakti, the Mother Goddess, Mother

Mary, or the divine feminine, among many other names. Our idea of the feminine goddess serves as our model for relationships with females, romantic or otherwise.

His mother had been cruel and abusive and seldom held him, and his hurt and anger at this became the basis for all further relationships. Quite simply, he selected women who prompted these emotional reactions within him. I asked him to imagine what the Divine Mother might really be like and embrace her as his "true" mother. The resulting second chakra shift worked. He has now been married to a lovely and kind woman—one who mirrors the qualities of the Divine, not the human mother—for several years.

CHAKRA ACTIVATION

Every chakra activates at a different time. During that time period, that chakra is "online." It is actively (and unconsciously) evaluating the worlds inside and outside the self in order to make conclusions about that chakra's concerns.

Your second chakra turns on between the age of six months and two and a half years. During these years, a child sleeps eight to ten hours a night, often in a fetal position. When awake, the young one is full of life, seeking to figure out their own feelings and needs in relationship with others. The body is a source of pleasure, as known through touch, taste, smell, sight, and hearing.

This chakra activates after the first chakra has turned on. Technically, the shift from one chakra to another occurs when the muladhara's element, which is earth, dissolves into the sacral chakra's element, which is water. A psychological change happens as the child now moves from self-absorption into bonding with family and friends. If a child's basic needs are met, it's time for them to become creative and enjoy the environment.

PSYCHOLOGICAL FUNCTIONS

As I shared earlier in this chapter, our sacral chakra is devoted to enabling us to bond. The most typical way of creating these inner and external relationships is through emotional empathy.

Everyone seeks to be understood. That phrase applies to the "selves within the self," such as our adult self with its inner children, and the "selves outside the self," such as other people, communities, and even natural beings, including animals. Allowing the sensing and sharing of our own feelings is key to recognizing our body's needs. Embracing others' feelings—without making them our own—leads to compassion and honesty.

With that in mind, we can approach our own feelings and those of others with grace. However, enjoying a healthy second chakra—and life—requires understanding the messages conveyed by the various feelings.

There are five basic feeling constellations, or families of feelings that convey messages we need to pay attention to.

ANGER: My boundaries are being violated, either by myself or someone or something else. I must establish a better boundary.

FEAR: There is something happening that is unsafe. I must move forward, backward, sidewise, or otherwise figure out how to become more secure.

DISGUST: Something or someone is bad for me. I must move away from or get rid of whatever it is.

SADNESS: I am not able to connect with love right now. It's important to perceive the love in a specific situation or go and create a more loving condition.

HAPPINESS: This is great! I want more of the same.

PSYCHOLOGICAL DEFICIENCIES IN AN UNHEALTHY SECOND CHAKRA

Let's say you're not doing so well psychologically in relation to your second chakra. There are many indicators that will clue you in to an imbalance.

Symptoms of deficiency in svadhisthana include rigidity in both body and beliefs, frigidity, self-denial, fear of change, and lack of social skills, desire, and creativity.

Symptoms of excess include addictions—to romance, sex, shopping, and some substances such as refined carbohydrates and wine—irresponsibility, codependency, emotionalism, invasiveness toward others, seductive manipulation, and obsessive attachments.

PSYCHOLOGICAL STRENGTHS
IN THE HEALTHY SECOND CHAKRA

When your second chakra is balanced and at ease, you'll experience friendliness, vitality, sensuality, and the ability to feel satisfied. You'll seek out life's emotional and physical pleasures, including those related to taste, touch, clothing choices, and just about everything else, without going overboard.

What about sexual expression? You don't have to participate in a sexual act to enjoy your sensuality. Go ahead. Select soaps, textures, even towels that affirm your love of the body. Not bogged down by bodily shame, you'll be able to easily decide what to indulge in and how far to take it.

Overall, you'll know to trust yourself when making decisions about relationships. Who is worthy of bonding with? Who is untrustworthy? No matter the type of connection, you'll be able to be yourself—carefree, emotionally solvent, and able to show your creative and sensitive self.

ASSOCIATED ARCHETYPES

An archetype is a template or model. There are positive and negative archetypes associated with your sacral chakra.

The positive archetype tied to svadhisthana is the emperor/empress. This template represents our inner ruler and our ability to bring our desires to fruition. The negative associated archetype is the martyr, who uses suffering to gain pity or establish control, yet can transform this tendency to live for a sacred cause. At all times, our sacral chakra and conscience ask us to decide whether to take responsibility for ourselves and our emotions or to abdicate the same and play the role of victim.

The following short exercise will help you sense the difference between operating as a ruler and a martyr.

PRACTICE

TRY ON YOUR
SECOND CHAKRA ARCHETYPES

Focus on a situation in which you need to make decisions or one that is causing an internal struggle. It could even be a relationship difficulty.

In a meditative and quiet state, imagine dealing with this situation through your chakra as an emperor or empress. How does that affect your sense of the situation and your assessment of yourself or any others involved? How does this attitude of self-relationship affect your approach to the circumstances?

Imagine yourself clearing that self-ruling energy and then focus again on your selected situation. Now you are going to try on the role of being a martyr. That's right: you are the victim. How does this mindset affect your perspective? What ideas does the victim mentality create as solutions to the problem?

Use the blue water of your second chakra to clean the martyrdom posture from your mind and body. Now make a definite choice between leaning into your issue as a ruler or a martyr.

PERSONALITY PROFILE

You might be someone highly gifted in your second chakra. The typical indicators of this include being quite sensitive to feelings. You are often the emotional heart of any crowd and that person everyone loves to tell their problems to. Be careful about that, though. You might be tempted to take care of others' needs instead of your own. You might also forget to pay attention to your own feelings, values, and sensual desires. Compassion starts and ends within—and toward—yourself.

You might also find it relatively easy to express yourself creatively. Do you paint, dance, or write poetry with wild abandon? Maybe you're that person who shares the most innovative point of view in the room. That slightly bohemian approach to reality adds joy and spice to the world.

Even if you are only minimally based in your watermoon chakra, emphasizing this aspect of yourself will add a little zip and zap to your life and relationships. After all, the basis of sensual enjoyment lies within the second chakra.

THE INTUITIVE GIFT
OF THE SECOND CHAKRA

For everyone, the second chakra is key to performing emotional empathy, which is the ability to sense in your body what is happening emotionally in someone else. For instance, if this chakra is tuned in, you might be able to tell if someone else is happy or sad. You can also distinguish between what they say they are feeling and what's really occurring inside them.

Think of how many times you've sat across a table from a friend and they have insisted they were A-OK. Meanwhile, deep inside your gut you absolutely know, without a doubt, that they are angry or upset. Your second chakra is always an accurate judge of what feelings truly exist within another living being.

Think about how helpful this gift is when you're interacting with someone you love. Is a family member in need? You can tune in. It even works with animals or plants. When this aptitude is turned on, you'll know that your pet is hungry or scared and that the plant needs water.

The downside of this attribute is that you can easily ignore your own feelings and needs in favor of others'. You might also just plain avoid your own issues, which can be the basis for selecting poor relationship partners or developing addictive tendencies, ranging from snacking on carbs (oh, the comfort those guarantee) to hiding from the world.

The following short exercise will help you practice separating your own feelings from those of others.

PRACTICE

EMOTIONAL EMPATHY: IS IT YOUR OWN FEELING OR SOMEONE ELSE'S?

You are feeling a feeling. That's great! As we've explored, if we interpret them accurately, all feelings enrich our lives—unless the feeling in your body belongs to someone else.

A few indicators that you are sensing another's feeling include the following:

» The feeling is too big for you.

» The feeling doesn't feel right—it just doesn't seem like it matches your personality.

» You're with another person and they seem to be denying their own emotions.

» You are hit out of the blue with an emotion for no apparent reason.

If you are struggling to determine if a feeling is your own or someone else's, you can walk through this short practice.

Breathe deeply into your sacrum and let your consciousness settle there. Attune to the feeling, and then make this statement aloud or internally:

Any feelings that are not my own
are now given back to them.

Then picture a bright blue river running through your second chakra from the back side of your sacral vertebrae to the front side. This water will dislodge and carry away any emotions that do not belong to you. It will request that the deity attending to the sacral chakra bring these emotions back to the true owners in a loving manner. Whatever remains will most likely be your own feeling. Act on its message in a smart way.

A FEW OTHER EXTRAORDINARY
SPIRITUAL ABILITIES

Besides emotional empathy, there are several additional spiritual capabilities that are often associated with a healthy and vibrant sacral chakra.

A handful of these are known as *siddhis*. This is a Hindu word that describes the powerful and magical abilities available through the second chakra when we've attained a high level of enlightenment or spiritual awareness. Tantric texts say that one who masters this chakra is safe from enemies and becomes like the sun, liberated from the darkness of their own ignorance. As well, the second chakra adept loses the fear of water and gains incredible numbers of psychic powers, along with control over the five senses. They also earn the full knowledge of astral entities and the ability to annihilate impurity. Eventually, it is said, the sacral chakra master conquers death.

There are yet other capabilities that are explained in more contemporary terms. We already covered emotional empathy, also called clairempathy. Other giftings include the following:

> » Claircognizance, or clear knowing, shows up through emotional clarity. For instance, we might simply know that someone is telling the truth or lying to us.

» Clairsentience, or clear sensing, occurs when our physical senses are stirred by psychic data. For instance, you might feel like someone not present is touching you, or you taste a food that your spouse will make for dinner that night. In particular, clairgustance is the ability to smell what isn't present, and clairtangency occurs when you can touch what isn't physically present.

» Claircoersion. Some individuals use their emotional sensitivity to manipulate others. It's relatively easy to persuade someone to do what is best for them—or maybe best for you—if you tune in to their emotions. It's called "pressing buttons," and there are a lot of ethics involved in applying this gift appropriately. It's never okay to alter someone's innermost values toward ends they wouldn't spiritually approve.

SUMMARY

The deep wellspring of your second chakra literally swims with psychological and spiritual attributes. Within the water-moon chakra are the roots of your five basic feelings, which serve as the foundation of your emotional well-being. First activated when you're quite young, this chakra's ability to support your relationships, sensuality, emotions, and creativity will be impacted, positively or negatively, by what occurs within and around you. Your reactions might very well cause you to operate from a martyr archetype rather than an emperor or empress archetype. Then again, there is always room to compensate for any psychological deficiencies and increase your psychological strengths by using the various intuitive gifts available through this energy center.

Ready to put all this knowledge to work? Part 2 will do just that.

PART 2

APPLYING SECOND CHAKRA
KNOWLEDGE IN REAL LIFE

• • • • • •

If you want to take a deep dive into the warm and joyful sea of your sacral chakra—into your emotions, creativity, and the font of inspiration—merge the moon together with the waters of love and life. You'll never be the same—in a good way.

Each of the following chapters is written by a different author. They are all knowledgeable about subtle energies, and each presents specific expertise that will leave you better informed and more empowered regarding your sacral chakra.

You can read these chapters in any order. If you want to better comprehend the physical nature of this sacral cauldron, skip to Dr. Nitin's chapter. If you are hungry and want to jump right into making a meal, there are two amazing chefs ready to walk you through second chakra recipes. Of course, you can always read the chapters in order and then change it up on your next time through.

YOU'LL BE USING INTENTION

To accelerate your second chakra growth and the emotive happiness linked with it, it's vital to understand how to shine a light on your desires and manifest them. We use the word *intention* to describe the method for coaxing our dreams into the 3D world. Intentions materialize when you merge your conscious, unconscious, and subconscious thoughts and feelings to activate your ability to manifest. This is how the world works, as does the making of a good life.

Many of the authors in this section will speak to the importance of intention. They will also provide you the means to declare and follow through on an intention. And it's okay to flounder a little at first. There are no mistakes in the energetic world—just opportunities to gather wisdom and flower.

The simplest way to compose an intention is to formulate a statement of desire. There are three basic parts to that equation. First, you engage a dream or need and phrase it in present time. Select positive, uplifting words, or negativity might strike—and you don't need that!

Next, feel that outcome as if it is already occurring. You want your mind and soul to meet in your body, which will encourage you to spot signs and take actions that will bring your desire to fruition.

The third step is to remind yourself about this decision. Declare it daily! Give yourself permission to roll it around in your head as often as you want. The more we call that desire forward, the surer it will happen.

Ready to try?

Think about something you'd like that relates to your second chakra: tasty food, colors, creativity, or emotional health. Pack that aspiration into a present-tense statement, like this:

> *I am wearing colors that fully*
> *express my internal spirit.*

Now go ahead and play with the feelings and movements of that affirmation. Wear it for a day or several days. When you notice a change in your behavior, perhaps create a secondary affirmation to match the first one, such as:

> *I am selecting all the colors of the rainbow*
> *as food to sustain a healthy body.*

Do you see how easy it is to create a future? Your sacral chakra is standing by to help.

4

SPIRIT ALLIES

MARGARET ANN LEMBO

Invisible allies are everywhere, in many forms. They are available to everyone and can show up upon request, so ask! But first, let's get familiar with the energies of these spirit helpers so you can be discerning and invite only those that will work for your highest good.

We all have an entourage of energetic assistants for all aspects of life. You can feel the essence of these helpers on a vibrational level. The best practice for attuning to your second chakra or for assisting it is telepathy: mind-to-mind and heart-to-heart communication using thoughts, feelings, and visualization to communicate with spirit allies.

Consider spirit allies in many forms, including angels and archangels, plant spirits, and the natural and fairy forces of essential oils, animal guides, and gemstone guardians. For more about the latter, you can refer to my section about working with crystals and gemstones in chapter 10.

Spirit allies influence us, and we receive guidance from all of nature. If we are open to it, it is easy to link with all life telepathically. The seen and unseen are real worlds, and these beings and energies help guide and light our path.

The sacral chakra is the chakra of activity, creativity, emotions, and fertility. With the help of your spirit allies, you can bring balance to your sacral chakra, act out your creative ideas, and forge a loving emotional reality. Toward that end, the next section provides descriptions of allies to connect with to commit to a goal, including affirmations you can use to work with each grouping.

Affirmations are empowering statements that use the tool of intention. As Cyndi explored in her beginning remarks on part 2, intention is easily packaged as affirmations that can be uttered internally or externally, sung or chanted, written, or even turned into poems to enforce a dream. They can also forge a bond with an ally or a collective of allies to assist you with gaining advice, lassoing their help, or learning a skill that they could teach you.

When set into an affirmation, an intention such as "I am now connecting with an angel" will invite that specific angelic love and support. If you were to use a phrase like "An angel is giving me a sign," you would open the portals between worlds so you can receive a message from that angel. The sacral chakra is especially potent when you formulate and employ intentions with deep feeling. After all, your water-moon chakra is all about intuition and emotion.

ANGELS AND ARCHANGELS

Angels and archangels are androgynous beings of light, color, and vibration, and they act and react based on your thoughts and your calls for assistance. They respond to prayers, requests, and petitions, serving as messengers of the Divine. They inspire each of us with guidance and wisdom. You can reach out to the following specific angels for sacral assistance.

Angel of Creative Intelligence

Because the sacral chakra is the chakra of creativity, align with the Angel of Creative Intelligence when you need to apply your knowledge and your skills to achieve your goals. This angel helps you access your full mental capacity and use your powers of reasoning and ingenuity to produce something unique. Ask this angel to help you increase your self-confidence, especially during times when you aren't feeling very smart or imaginative.

Send off a little petition to this angel to officially ask for assistance. Something like this:

O Angel of Creative Intelligence! Please show me
how to develop my inner genius. Guide me to educate

myself in areas where my knowledge is lacking.
Help me tap into the divine wisdom I need to
accomplish whatever I put my mind to. Thank you!

Then apply any one of the following affirmations to continue the forward movement this angel has provided.

AFFIRMATIONS: I complete my tasks and creative projects with ease. I'm self-motivated and productive. I am an intelligent being with the ability to focus on complex tasks. Creativity flows through me. I am courageous, and I bravely bring my ideas into actuality. My imagination is the key to my success.

Angel of Emotional Balance

When you find yourself acting out like a child or feeling emotionally out of balance, call on the Angel of Emotional Balance. Ask this angel to help you realign at times when you realize that you've been treating others disrespectfully or acting immaturely. The sacral chakra holds emotions that have been shoved down and not dealt with. These emotions will bubble up when someone or something triggers them. It can be as if someone pushed a button, and emotions run rampant as a result.

Ask for guidance and let this angel help you determine if you are experiencing emotional exhaustion due to life changes, a medical condition, overwork, or financial stress. Look at the part you played in the actions of others, and their reactions to you, to help discover how to improve yourself. Take steps to make the shift necessary to be happy.

Remember that you create your own reality, so use the following types of affirmations to continue your progress.

AFFIRMATIONS: My emotions are balanced. Events from my past positively affect my present and future because I have released any negative emotional charge and see only the lessons learned.

Angel of Fertility

Being fertile for reproduction is only one aspect of fertility. Fertility and manifesting what you want to create in your world are associated with the sacral chakra. Call on the Angel of Fertility to support you whether you want to have a child or cultivate a fertile mind. Turn to this angel when you are ready to give birth to your creative ideas. Manifesting what you create in your imagination takes great courage and long-term dedication. Whether you want to be fertile to carry a new life or an idea, this angel is your ally.

Make a special request, prayer, or petition to the Angel of Fertility to align with creative inspiration. Ask for help to embrace your imagination and be self-motivated or align yourself with your unborn child to connect with the spirit of the baby and bring the child into manifest reality.

The following types of affirmations can continue this good work.

AFFIRMATIONS: I am fertile in body, mind, and soul. My body is ripe to give birth figuratively or literally. Vital life force flows vibrantly through me. I am strong and healthy. I am extremely creative and imaginative.

Archangel Gabriel

Responsible for the birth order of souls, Archangel Gabriel watches over unborn children as they come to term in utero and whispers to them all the knowledge of heaven. As the baby is born, Gabriel seals the secret in each child by pressing the baby's lips, leaving a soft mark that appears as a cleft beneath the nose.

Because Gabriel watches over unborn children, you can call on the Angel of Childbirth for help in the mental, emotional, and spiritual processes that you will go through to become a parent, if or when you are preparing to conceive.

With the sacral chakra as the center for creativity, call on Archangel Gabriel for inspired guidance and to open your spiritual ears to hear messages and advice, often through symbols and dreams.

Use these types of affirmations to accelerate your desires:

AFFIRMATIONS: I receive messages every day in every way. I interpret the signs from above with great accuracy. Guidance and inspiration from my angels and other spirit guides comes to me moment by moment.

Archangel Jehudiel

Archangel Jehudiel makes a good spirit ally to help you fulfill your important mission. Call on them when you want assistance with discovering and accomplishing your spiritual soul's purpose. Let them shine their light to find the career that is best for you and your reason for being here so you can use your sacral chakra's creative energy to manifest your true purpose. Ask Jehudiel to remove any perceived blocks or emotional challenges from your path. Use their energy to protect you so you can accomplish what you are meant to do, and draw on the following types of affirmations:

AFFIRMATIONS: I'm self-motivated and productive. I complete my tasks and creative projects with ease. I am grateful for all my creative and business skills. I earn unlimited income doing what I love.

ANIMAL GUIDES

At any moment, we can call upon the animals as well as other species of nature to bring us a sign, deliver information, help us solve a knotty problem, or convey their unique traits for our use. An animal guide just might show up in everyday reality, such as through the appearance of an actual animal or nature being. Then again, they can also visit us intuitively, such as through night dreams, daydreams, or psychic visions. Following are several examples of natural beings that could show up to provide insight for a sacral chakra need.

Bee

Call on the energy of Bee if you are trying to get pregnant or come up with a new idea. Align with the energy of Bee when you are working toward reproducing or producing a fruitful outcome. When Bee shows up in your life, it is time to cultivate concepts or projects through action. Do what needs to be done, and make things happen. It's time to be productive! Develop your own affirmations or consider these:

AFFIRMATIONS: I am fertile with great ideas. I am
focused and creative. It is easy for me to be
creative and bring a project to fruition. Building
and creating are joyful experiences for me.

Dragonfly

Dragonfly is an ally that can help you see life with great
clarity and take action. Dragonfly is symbolic of pure water,
and water symbolizes uncovering and understanding emotions and feelings. When Dragonfly appears in your life, it
is time to awaken and recognize your emotions and feelings
and then take rapid action to create the life you want. Ask
yourself what you want. Define your desires and get going. It is your life. You create it with your thoughts, feelings,
words, and actions, employing affirmations like these:

AFFIRMATIONS: It's easy for me to maintain
balanced emotions. I pay attention to my
dreams, interpret them, and then act based on
my findings. My understanding of symbols
helps increase my self-awareness and supports
me as I take action to design my reality.

Rabbit

Rabbit hops into your life to teach you the power of co-
creation and the energy of being still. Rabbit teaches you
to wait one moon cycle (about twenty-eight days) to allow

your answers to be revealed. This is also the cycle associated with menstruation, which aligns with the physical aspect of the sacral chakra. You will know in which direction to move after you pause for contemplation. The message is to stop, observe, go within, and then be mindful of when it is best to move forward again. As you do so, use this vibe to contemplate what fertility means to you. Whether you are preparing for literal birth or for the proliferation of ideas and the ability to birth them into manifest reality, Rabbit can be your ally to bring good energy into manifesting your reality.

Let Rabbit assist you with statements like these:

AFFIRMATIONS: It is easy for me to give birth to ideas. There are infinite possibilities available to all beings. My creative endeavors come to fruition. I easily hop forward with renewed clarity. I find balance within the cycles of life.

FAIRY AND OTHER NATURAL FORCES

The natural world is alive with beings and forces that would love to assist us with our sacral chakra desires, from innovating within our career to soothing hurt feelings. Many of these beings belong to the fairy realm, which is also called the devic kingdom. These spirits might help guide you toward an herb or other plant, or an essential oil composed of a natural substance.

Essential oils are created from any number of natural products, including flower petals and parts such as leaves, bark, roots, rinds, seeds, and more. How can you best work with an essential oil? There are many ways.

One method is to drip two or three drops of an essential oil into a neutral carrier like almond oil. You want to dilute the oil so it's between 1 and 5 percent oil. You can then apply the liquid topically.

You can inhale an oil directly or put a few drops in a bath or on a warm or cold compress. You can also smell an essential oil using a diffuser that disperses it into the air.

Be careful with essential oils! They can be harmful if you're allergic to a specific oil, and some oils can cause internal or external reactions. Always check with a doctor if you are dealing with challenges or using medicines that could conflict with an essential oil.

Following are several of my favorite essential oils that I believe are perfect for providing sacral chakra support.

Clary Sage Essential Oil

Clary sage relaxes, comforts, and grounds feelings and emotions. It replaces the energy of hysteria with a sense of well-being and euphoria. It is especially beneficial when emotions are running rampant. Use it for calming and releasing anger and frustration. It helps quell emotional outbursts brought on by premenstrual syndrome, menopause, and other hormone-related upsets. This essential oil helps you acknowledge and accept hormone-related realizations as accurate but also helps you find a way to deal with and express them in a way that other people can handle.

Affirmations like the following can assist you on the clary sage path:

AFFIRMATIONS: I embrace my emotions as I allow balance to return to my life. Nurturing energy surrounds me, bringing my emotional body into alignment. I have the courage to step forward with joy and enthusiasm.

FOR YOUR SAFETY: Clary sage has a sedative effect; avoid prior to driving and when it is necessary to stay alert. Avoid when drinking alcohol, as nausea may result. Do not use if pregnant or nursing.

Juniper Berry Essential Oil

Juniper berry improves your potential to deal with your feelings and emotional difficulties. Inhale this essential oil and visualize a restoration of inner harmony and self-confidence. It is beneficial when you want to break ties to anything that is holding you back from living a happy and fulfilled life.

Call upon juniper berry with these types of statements:

AFFIRMATIONS: My emotions are balanced, and I
enjoy this state of being. Events from my past
positively affect my present and future. I embrace
change. I recognize that change can usher in
improved life situations, which starts with my
thoughts and where I place my focus.

FOR YOUR SAFETY: Avoid use in cases of kidney
disease. Do not use if pregnant or nursing.

Petitgrain Essential Oil

Petitgrain shines light on mental obstacles. Use this essential oil for manifesting and activating the power of the emotional mind to create reality. This essential oil activates creative thought processes, helping you bring forth inspiration. It calms feeling-based strain, relieves mental stress, supports intellectual activity, and affirms a positive approach to sticky situations.

Especially supportive are these types of affirmations:

AFFIRMATIONS: I'm self-motivated to be productive.
My tasks and creative projects are completed with
ease. I am a caretaker of the earth, and I take the
time to enjoy nature.

Ylang-Ylang Essential Oil

Ylang-ylang is an aphrodisiac and is beneficial in fertility blends. (Your sacral chakra loves anything that increases fertility of all sorts!) Due to its stress-reducing properties, it lowers blood pressure, helps improve sleep patterns, and reduces feelings of being overwhelmed.

Embrace ylang-ylang with affirmations like these.

AFFIRMATIONS: All I need is always within reach.
I am grateful for everything I have. Extraordinary love and amazing wealth on all levels are always available to me.

FOR YOUR SAFETY: Avoid use in cases of low blood pressure. Do not use if pregnant or nursing.

As you work with each of these spirit allies, use them to improve your awareness. When one or more of your chakras becomes blocked or out of alignment, your mental state or your emotional balance is affected. A blocked chakra can also affect you spiritually. Eventually, the blockage presents itself on the physical level in the form of disease or some health condition that seems to show up out of nowhere. However, the block or lack of well-being didn't come from nowhere. Let yourself work with the underlying issues so you can keep on shining.

SUMMARY

Self-awareness and being truly conscious of sacral chakra ideas, feelings, and actions can shift your reality and lead you to a deeply positive life experience. The beings and spirits you met in this chapter are always here to help.

5

YOGA POSES

AMANDA HUGGINS

I vividly remember the first time I heard someone cry in a yoga class.

It was over a decade ago. The teacher had us resting in pigeon pose, a deep hip stretch. Though my head was down and my eyes were shut, I could hear the distinct sniffling and deep breathing of the young woman next to me. I could tell she was crying, but I wasn't sure why. I assumed she must have just been having a bad day.

The more yoga classes I attended, the more often I noticed that other yogis also seemed to have the occasional cry during class. I'd hear a little snuffle, a deep sigh, a sharp inhale from a fellow student . . . and it almost always occurred during a deep hip stretch. *Surely they weren't all having a bad day!* I thought. There had to be another reason for the emotional release.

I was still quite new to yoga at the time, and I wasn't yet aware of the profound connection between our physical and energetic bodies. I started to understand when it happened to me.

I was taking a yin yoga class, a slow-paced practice that entails long holds in restorative yoga poses. The instructor had us in a hip stretch for about four minutes. At first it was no big deal. After the first minute or two, I began to feel an enormous amount of resistance building in my hips. The discomfort was all I could focus on, so to dissolve my resistance, I drew my attention back to my breathing. Rather than fight the sensations, I deepened my exhalations, surrendering into the sensations. As I breathed deeply and sat with my battle, a wave of emotion washed over me. Out of nowhere, I began to cry. I wasn't particularly sad; it felt more like a gentle release.

Why did that happen during a hip stretch, and what's that got to do with the second chakra?

The hips are the largest weight-bearing joints in the body. They allow us to sit, stand, squat, and get into funky yoga poses from time to time. The hip flexors can also be activated, consciously or unconsciously, when we are in fight-or-flight mode. Stressful or traumatic experiences can cause the hip muscles, specifically the psoas muscles, to go into flexion as the body's protective mechanism. This creates both a physical and an emotional signature in the body. If the hips and surrounding areas aren't given an opportunity to release the tension, it continues to accumulate over time and gets stored in the body.

All this happens in the space where our energetic body stores emotional stress: the sacral chakra. In fact, some yoga teachers refer to the hips and sacral area as the body's "emotional junk drawer"! A mindful yoga practice is a fantastic tool for energetically cleaning out that drawer.

SACRAL CHAKRA YOGA FOR PHYSICAL AND EMOTIONAL RELEASE

If life is a video game, yoga is a "cheat code" for activating the chakra system. When you're engaged in a posture— breathing deeply and drawing focus to the space where you're feeling the stretching, resistance, or challenge— you're naturally connecting with your energy centers. I find that this is especially true for the sacral chakra because so many wonderful poses draw attention and energy to the hips and sacral space.

The way you relate to hip stretches in yoga may serve as a good mirror for the way you relate to your life emotions. For example, when a pose becomes challenging, do you want to run away or get out of it as fast as you can? Do you grit your teeth and tense up? Do you find that frustration—or even anger—bubbles up to the surface?

Perhaps you're able to notice the discomfort without allowing it to swallow you whole. Do you choose to breathe deeply and surrender into the pose, acknowledge the challenge, and ultimately release more deeply into it?

The latter choice, which is one of witnessing, surrender, and release, doesn't circumvent the challenge of the pose. Rather, it offers ease within mind and body to work *through* the difficulty.

Our ability to practice emotional release is similar. Before moving forward from a triggering, stressful, or traumatic experience, we need to fully witness the spectrum of emotions we're feeling. Perhaps you've heard the phrase "Feel it to heal it," which encourages us to witness, honor, and hold space for the pain so we might then release and heal.

You don't necessarily need to know what you're releasing every time you're practicing a sacral chakra pose in yoga. Some days you might: perhaps you've been feeling emotionally low or shut down, or you've been revisiting a past experience laden with shadowy emotions. But if you're not able to connect with a specific memory or "thing" to release, that's perfectly fine. I encourage you to view the idea of release in a more general sense: *I am releasing all the thoughts, feelings, and emotions that no longer serve me.*

I love blending sacral chakra work and yoga because that chakra is the epicenter of physical and emotional release. And as we clear out physical and energetic space in the second chakra, we're able to welcome a more grounded, creative, and connected emotional expression.

CREATIVE EXPRESSION THROUGH THE SECOND CHAKRA

Yoga is a naturally creative practice. While there are specific poses and alignment cues within the practice, there is also an infinite amount of freedom for self-expression within (and in between) each pose.

When I first began practicing yoga, I was fixated on doing each pose "right." As I grew more comfortable within my practice and my body, I began to realize how much fun it could be to play with my practice as a vehicle for self-expression. Sometimes my yoga feels like a dance or a song or making love to myself. Sometimes it feels like a sacred, solemn expression of power. Other days it's a soulful and mindfully slow practice of honoring and releasing any emotions or memories it's time to let go of.

Because the second chakra is also the home of creativity, expression, and sexual energy, it's a wonderful way to explore those spaces on your mat. The next time you roll out your mat to practice, I encourage you to tune in deeply to yourself, connect with your second chakra, and reflect on any version of the following questions:

> » How do I want to express myself through my practice right now?

> » What poses, shapes, or movements would feel absolutely delicious today?

> » How can I alchemize my feelings, my movement, and my creativity through today's practice?

Allow your intuitive wisdom to guide your practice.

PRACTICE

ACTIVATING THE SECOND CHAKRA IN YOGA

Before we explore a yoga sequence to activate the second chakra, I'd like to focus on a simple restorative posture that will begin to awaken the second chakra: the supine spinal twist. The simplicity of the pose will allow you to draw attention to the second chakra, and it feels great! I love to start and end my day with supine twists; they're my favorite way to stretch, connect with my energy, and enjoy a moment of release.

Twists offer fantastic visuals. They are equivalent to wringing out an old washcloth that's accumulated dirt. You're squeezing out the resistance, tension, and emotion that no longer serve you. The more you're able to breathe, draw attention to your sacral chakra, and surrender, the deeper into the pose you'll find yourself.

You might notice that your twists feel a little different from day to day. Sometimes you may have more depth and space, while at other times you'll notice resistance or tension in the body. Twisting is a beautiful, continually unfolding experience that asks you to meet yourself where you are and surrender into your current experience.

How to Practice Supine Spinal Twists

Lie on your mat in *savasana,* or corpse pose, then hug both knees to your chest and breathe deeply.

To do the spinal twist, bring your arms out into a T shape on your mat with palms facing down and find a soft concentration in your sacral chakra. As you exhale, slowly drop both knees to one side. Keep your shoulders flat on the floor, close your eyes, and relax into the pose. With eyes closed, connect with your second chakra and breathe deeply.

Notice if any physical or emotional resistance builds. Continue softening, releasing, and surrendering into the shape of the pose. Stay for five to ten cycles of breath before switching sides.

For a modification that doesn't involve getting down on the floor, try seated savasana. Sitting in a chair, rest your hands in your lap and allow your eyes to close. Let go of any tension in the body and simply receive the restorative benefits of relaxation. You can also put a pillow underneath your feet if you want to.

To perform a seated spinal twist, sit upright on the edge of a chair, spine elongated, feet flat on the floor. Place your right hand on the right edge of the chair behind you and place your left arm on your right thigh just above your knee. Inhale. Exhale as you gently twist to the right as far as is comfortable. Lead with your shoulders and the head and neck will come along for the ride. Inhale and lift your spine up, out of your hips. Exhale and twist a little farther. Hold for a few seconds. Release and repeat these steps on the other side, gently twisting to the left.

PRACTICE

FULL YOGA SEQUENCE TO ACTIVATE YOUR SECOND CHAKRA

Before you engage in the following yoga flow, pause and connect with an intention regarding your second chakra.

You may want to ask yourself: *Is there anything that wants to be released today? Will that release create more space for me to express? How or what would I like to express through my practice today?* Notice what comes up, then allow the wisdom of your second chakra to guide your practice.

I also encourage you to take a few minutes to warm up the body. Because so many of these poses are focused on the hip joints, it's important to prepare your muscles and gently increase the range of motion in the lower body. Engaging in a brief warm-up routine will not only reduce the risk of injury but also enhance your overall practice, allowing you to fully enjoy the benefits of the poses.

To warm up, you may choose to practice some traditional sun salutations or simply warm up with some light stretching. One simple warm-up stretch is to lay flat on your back and hug your knees to your chest. With your hands holding on to your knees, gently guide your hips in circles, moving both clockwise and counterclockwise.

After you've adequately warmed up the hips, find a downward-facing dog on your mat.

» Downward-facing dog

Begin on your hands and knees. Your hands should be shoulder-width apart and knees hip-width apart.

Tuck your toes, lift your knees off the ground, and straighten your legs, forming an inverted V shape with your body. Press your palms into the ground and relax your head and neck between your arms.

Peddle out your feet to stretch the backs of the legs, and then find stillness. Stay here for five breaths. On each inhale, draw energy from the feet, up the legs, and into the sacral chakra. On each exhale, sink your roots deeper into the earth. Find stability, then step or jump to the front of your mat.

Modification: You may skip downward-facing dog altogether if mobility is limited. Instead, practice seated inhalations and exhalations. As you breathe in, draw your arms up to the sky to find length. As you breathe out, bring your hands to your heart center, palms together. Find the balance and stability here.

Modification: Seated sun salutation with chair. You can do sun salutations with a chair for additional support. Stand in front of the chair with your palms together at your heart center. Inhale and raise your arms. As you exhale, lean forward and rest your palms on the back of the chair. Inhale, straighten your arms, grasp the chair back with both hands, move your left foot backward and bend your right knee. On the next inhale, move your right foot back to meet your left, and then exhale and bend slightly forward. Move up onto your tiptoes and stand, straightening your arms, still grasping the chair. Switch sides and repeat.

> » Warrior 2

Stand facing the long side of your mat with your feet wide apart. Angle the toes of your left foot to point slightly toward the front of your mat. Point the toes of your right foot toward the front of the mat. Press the four corners of your feet down, and root to rise. Inhale and raise your arms parallel to the floor, with shoulders down and neck long. Bend your right knee. Stay here for three to five cycles of breath. With every inhale, draw length and strength up through the sacral chakra; with every exhale, create more grounding as you drop deeper into the pose. Repeat on the other side.

Modification: You may substitute with gentle seated twists. Inhale and reach your arms to the sky. As you exhale, bring your arms parallel to the ground and twist to the left. Repeat on the other side.

> » Reverse warrior

Keep the lower body exactly as it is in warrior 2. Place your back arm alongside your back leg. Inhale and lift your front arm up and overhead behind you, creating a stretch along the side of your upper body.

Holding this pose following warrior 2 will likely bring up resistance in the legs and sacral area. Continue using the breath to release, surrender, and remain in the discomfort as best you can.

Inhale and bring both legs together, then repeat on the other side.

» Bridge pose

Lie down on your back on the mat. Bend your knees and plant both feet on the mat, hip-width apart. Rest your arms beside the body with palms facing down. As you inhale, connect with the sacral chakra and lift your hips up toward the sky. The feet will remain rooted into the earth for support. Breathe into—and send energy through—the second chakra for two to three cycles of breath. Gently release the hips back down to the ground. Find a moment to reset, then repeat twice more.

Modification: While performing bridge pose, put a yoga block under your sacrum and rest your arms above your head.

» Reclined butterfly pose

Lie on your back with knees bent. Exhale and bring the soles of the feet to touch one another, allowing the knees to splay out to either side of the body. Allow the second chakra to shine as you breathe directly into the hips and lower belly. Keeping the body and breath soft, envision any excess emotions, thoughts, or energy draining out of the second chakra and into the ground. Stay here for about thirty to sixty seconds, or longer if you'd like. When you're ready to continue, bring the knees together and hug them into the chest.

Modification: If there's too much intensity in the hips doing the pose as outlined, you may use blocks or pillows underneath the knees for support.

» Spinal twists

Practice spinal twists on both sides.

» Savasana

Close the practice by lying on the floor with the palms facing up. Allow the earth beneath you to support the entirety of your body weight. Let the breath's natural rhythm arise. You may choose to envision the color orange as you softly breathe, rest, and restore. Stay here for as long as you'd like.

Modification: In seated savasana, allow the eyes to close and rest your hands with palms facing down in your lap. Let go of any tension in the body and simply receive the restorative benefits of relaxation.

Close with the mantra "I feel peace."

SUMMARY

Yoga is meant to be enjoyed, which is key to creating a healthy second chakra. Above all, please remember that the wisdom of your second chakra lies within you. Let the feeling of flow serve as a guide while you allow your own creative expression and release to work through you.

6

BODY WISDOM

NITIN BHATNAGAR, DO

As a cardiologist, I recognize that I'm in rare company when writing about chakras. The allopathic medical community I am a part of doesn't usually refer to the chakras, much less the other subtle energy structures. But I'm convinced of the importance of these powerful organs to those seeking to understand their true selves and improve their physical health.

In this chapter I'll delve into sacral chakra knowledge to assist you in improving your overall bodily well-being. How might you harness this creative, emotionally available chakra? I'll provide knowledge, advice, and practices to help you do just that.

THE POWER OF CHAKRAS
TO SUPPORT YOUR BODY

Each chakra operates like a charged battery, transmitting its own unique energy throughout your body. Every chakra also connects to a corresponding organ system via a complex conduit of nerve fibers that emanate from the spinal cord. When a chakra is disrupted, the result is stagnation in that organ system. Over time, the resulting lack of efficiency can lead to disease and hormonal imbalances. For this reason, it is essential to take care of each chakra so it can create health within its own area of expertise and contribute to the well-being of the entire self.

Interestingly, we can observe the presence of an illness and infer corresponding chakra disturbances. Which set of symptoms relates to which chakra? By answering this query and tracking a set of issues to its most likely chakra, we can make corrections to heal the "off" chakra and restore balance. This reinvigorates the flow of energy along the energy system of the nadis, which are often associated with the nerves, and harmonizes the related organ system with all other structures for optimal functioning.

SECOND CHAKRA ANATOMY AND
BASIC PHYSICAL FUNCTIONS

To engineer your second chakra to be more balanced, it helps to get oriented to its physical location and functions. While some of the information that follows is also found in part 1, reviewing it here will give you the broadest possible understanding of your sacral chakra.

Your second chakra lies between the coccyx and the sacrum, approximately two inches below the navel. Its reach extends to the nerve plexus of your pelvic region, establishing its essential role in influencing your sex organs: the testes and the ovaries.

It's not just about sex, though. The second chakra also directs the gastrointestinal system and many other systems and functions. The sacral chakra is home to your enteric nervous system, which is also called the gut or second brain. (Yes, there is a brain down there!) Scientists and medical professionals now know that we have three "brains." Each employs its own form of intelligence to help us navigate life. You are obviously acquainted with the brain in your head: your thinking brain. The heart has its own nervous system too and demonstrates a unique intellect, emotionally and physically; think of it as your spiritual brain. The gut brain is equally significant in that it regulates much of your immune system, digestive processes, and emotions, and serves as a chief input for your autonomic nervous system. I call it the reactive brain.

Your autonomic nervous system consists of the enteric, parasympathetic, and sympathetic nervous systems. The parasympathetic oversees resting and digesting, and the sympathetic speeds you up. Together, all three systems form the polyvagal system, which is served by the vagus nerve. The vagus nerve tells you whether you are stressed or not, based on internal programs. Most of the messages flowing from your gut brain to your thinking brain are carried upward from the gut brain through the heart brain and into the head brain.

As I noted, the sacral chakra's far-reaching influence is largely invested in the reproductive system. The testes produce testosterone, and the ovaries produce estrogen and progesterone. These sex hormones influence our fertility, emotions, and inherent personalities. When the hormones are out of balance, we can experience instability in all areas of life.

I must also mention a few other important second chakra organs. The sacral chakra's influence includes the uterus, fallopian tubes, and other reproductive organs. It also includes the prostate gland, a small organ that sits below the bladder and controls the flow of urine and the creation of semen.

HOW YOUR SECOND CHAKRA
IMPACTS YOUR PHYSICAL HEALTH

We have seen that much of our physical wellness is contingent on boosting and maintaining a healthy sacral area. Let's first return to the second chakra's role in gastrointestinal activity. The enteric nervous system occupies a primary role in immunity, emotional response, stress reactions, neurological performance, and more. That's why when the sacral chakra is impeded, your very vitality is jeopardized, threatening your health and even your decision-making abilities. Symptoms can involve any of the organs or systems in the sacral area and even the bones and muscles there. You might experience intestinal disorders, reproductive problems, autoimmune conditions, or even neurological imbalances. A long list of sexual problems can originate from sacral chakra imbalances, including infertility, erectile dysfunction, and ejaculatory impotence.

We never quite know whether an issue has originated from an imbalanced chakra or a chakra's balance has been thrown off by physical or psychological conditions. A few of the more measurable or medically understood causes of sacral chakra issues can include alcoholism, drug addiction, endocrine and neurological diseases, anxiety, stress, depression, and vascular dysfunction. These types of problems can often be diagnosed by a health care provider through testing and sometimes by healers trained in the art of chakra healing and energy medicine. Always defer to evaluations made by licensed professionals.

YOUR SECOND CHAKRA AND YOUR PSYCHOLOGICAL WELFARE

The whole body pulsates with the vibrational frequency of the sacral chakra. A healthy second chakra is evidenced by your ability to fully embrace and enjoy the "good life." Other indicators of a functional sacral chakra include feeling emotionally satisfied, uninhibited within your relationships, and confident in intimacy. When your gut, reproductive, and related neurological systems are all functional, you'll be filled with joy and satisfied in your daily endeavors.

The roles that sensuality and sexuality play in your life are largely determined by the balance of the sacral chakra. Basically, these aspects are life enhancing if you're expressing your highest creative values. They can be disabling for many reasons, such as if you're perceiving unrealistic expectations from a partner or perhaps projecting unmanageable expectations onto them. Fantastical anticipations on either side create disharmony within the mind as well as the hormones and emotions. Holding inaccurate or impossible notions of masculinity, femininity, strength, and beauty (or lack thereof) can also cause polarizations in the mind and body.

In general, when the chakra is overfunctioning, you might develop addictive behaviors, act irresponsibly, and become afflicted with obsessions and codependency. You could also experience a constant state of overwhelm and mood swings. When the chakra is underfunctioning or operating in a deficit, you can fall prey to self-denial and inflexibility. The resulting lack of imagination and creativity can also cause emotional unresponsiveness, leading to poorly operating immune, digestive, or neurological systems.

Additional psychological problems can result from sacral chakra imbalances. Conditions like premature or rapid ejaculation and impotence may be linked with physical pathologies, such as a stasis of sexual energy in the pelvic musculature, but they might also be influenced by perceptions held within the second chakra, as well as second chakra–oriented emotional stress, lack of confidence, or unresolved conflicts.

While prostate issues can certainly originate with physical issues related to that gland, such as infections or cancer, emotional factors could underlie them. The metaphysical analogy that most often underlies prostate problems is the inability to allow the flow of creativity. Factors blocking that free flow might include misperceptions about life, anxiety, stress, and a lack of clear vision and goals. When the prostate negatively impacts semen production, it's important to become aware of your divinely given right to birth creative ideas.

When your enteric nervous system is negatively impacting your overall health or factors linked to polyvagal function, you might lack a sense of life purpose or maybe you "can't get it up"! That can happen to everybody, actually, and the solution is the same: embrace a sense of meaning, and align with your highest values and creativity.

Do You Have Second Chakra Issues?

Following is a list of conditions that might point to this chakra as their origin:

- » intestinal or other gastric issues

- » reproductive or sexual hormone problems

- » pelvic floor or sacrum pain or challenges

- » immune disorders or inconsistencies

- » under- or overreacting to stress

- » emotional imbalances

- » sensuality or sexuality dysfunction

- » craving for comfort food

- » anxiety or depression

» intimacy challenges

» an eating disorder

» additional challenges in any of the second chakra systems or bodily parts explored in part 1

A FEW EASY WAYS TO SUPPORT YOUR SECOND CHAKRA

DANCE. It doesn't matter if you are a so-called "good" dancer or not. Anytime you move around, whether to music vibrating through the air or the music of your mind, you are activating your sacral chakra.

WATER. Connecting with water is vital to restoring the flow of your water-moon chakra. Hydrate all day long to bathe your cells and organ systems with the key nutrient of water. You can also swim in open water or even take an extra shower or bath.

SECOND CHAKRA FOODS. To fuel your second chakra, feed it what it really loves: orange foods and comfort foods. Try squashes, salmon, nuts, oranges . . . you get it.

COLOR THERAPY. Since the root chakra is associated with orange, how about wearing orange clothes?

That will pick you up and bring a smile deep within your sacral self.

FEEL YOUR FEELINGS. Feelings are the messengers of your sacral chakra. Let them arise, and fruitfully express them: anger, fear, sadness, disgust, joy—there is a place for them all. But be responsible. Just as you don't want your feelings to implode inside you, neither should they explode at anyone else.

CREATE. Get your creative energy flowing through vibrant expression. Tap into your inner muse in any way that works for you: try music, art, or writing. You can also cook, draw, garden, or take on a new creative hobby.

PRACTICE

OPENING YOUR SACRUM

I already advised you to open your sacrum through dance. Well, there is more than one way to move those hips, isn't there?

Anytime you move your sacrum, you are releasing negative emotions and issues and summoning the types of subtle energies you need to be emotive, creative, and full of self-love. This short practice—a literal exercise—will free your sacral chakra and invite joy.

» Begin by focusing on an issue that you believe originates in your sacral chakra. It might involve your gastrointestinal or reproductive system, your nerves and stress reactions, emotional or intimacy needs, sexuality, or just about anything else related to your ability to love yourself.

» Either standing or seated, whichever you prefer, put your hands on your abdomen. Breathe deeply, feeling the ebb and flow of energy in your sacral area. Then imagine that you are filling that bodily area, front and back, with a bright shade of orange. Let that orange spread through your hips and belly, and then upward through your spine, by moving gently. You might swing, dance, sway, or otherwise create vibration through your body. Be sure to invite your legs and arms into the flow. Stop when you sense that the orange color is expanding beyond your physical form and enveloping your entire self, and you feel calm and at ease.

A SVADHISTHANA MUDRA

Mudras can assist in expanding and cleansing your sacral chakra. Hand mudras are a special feature of tantric Buddhism and are also used in Indian classical dance. Medieval hatha yoga texts, which describe physical yoga poses, are a major source of information about mudras. I recommend you employ the Shakti Mudra, also called the Gesture of the Divine Feminine or the Gesture of Power, to bring feminine and creative life-force energy into your sacral chakra (see figure 2).

FIGURE 2: SHAKTI MUDRA

To perform this mudra, follow these steps:

Bring your palms together prayerfully at your heart. Breathe deeply. Tuck your thumbs into the palms of your hands. Fold your index fingers and middle fingers over the tops of your thumbs, knuckles touching. Bring the tips of your ring fingers and little fingers together so they touch. You can either allow the base of your palms to touch or not. Hold this mudra in front of your heart for several minutes. If your arms get tired, you can rest your closed hands on your abdomen for three or more minutes in addition to the time spent at your heart.

SUMMARY

Your sacral chakra is intertwined with all levels of your physical self, its health often determining the well-being of most of your organ systems as well as your relational and emotional selves. Having gained a fuller understanding of this chakra's role in your life, and by adopting some of the practices and other tips offered here, you will be able to move more readily and more often into states of ease and joy.

7

SELF-HEALING AND GROUNDING

AMELIA VOGLER

I spent my early life playing in the creek, pond, fields, and woodlands of our family farm and visiting the funeral home that has been in my family for more than 250 years and counting—from before the United States Constitution was ratified.

My family seems to have always cared for the dead and those grieving them, learning how to be in relationship with the everlasting Spirit. Creator birthed me (or perhaps I chose to be birthed—wink, wink) in the perfect family and environment to nurture my whimsical, sensitive, healing nature—which, I've come to find out, is very connected to the water-moon chakra.

I am fortunate. My childhood was intimately connected to the delicate harmony of nature and the healing power of balance. I watched cloud circuses dance animals, people, and fairies across the sky; studied the changing seasons; and ate berries, green beans, and peppers growing from rich soil in the garden. I woke every morning to the sun-kissed pond reflecting rippling waves on my ceiling. I was safe enough to develop the ability to see and sense energy—to feel deeply, as we do through the sacral chakra.

And then I went to school.

Dyslexic and struggling to read, larger bodied than my peers, and "a farm girl," I was bullied and an outcast. My childhood became a constant negotiation between staying open, being one with the larger waltz of life, and closing off, blocking my feelings to avoid being hurt. *To feel or not to feel* became my soul's most important question.

Today I help individuals feel whole again and reengage with the parts of themselves they have shut down. In doing this work, I energetically empathize with my clients. I feel what they feel. These feelings—the sensations, the emotions—are the language the second chakra uses to communicate the soul's messages and desires. These feelings become an essential map for personal healing.

This chapter dives into practices and exercises to support the relationship between your soul and its language of feeling. Here you will continue to ground yourself as a healer by expanding the core foundations of self-healing and awakening the balanced potential of your sacral chakra through both hands-on and experiential practices.

FOUNDATIONS FOR SELF-HEALING

The provision for healing that is available through the second chakra is to show up in the present moment. When working with the sacral chakra, you often work in the sphere of emotions, especially those that are easy to overlook. As you experiment with the practices I will guide you through, call upon your courageous and curious personal spirit. Meet these practices with honesty, for there is nothing to be embarrassed about. We are all walking, dancing, trying, and faltering.

Perhaps many parts of your life seem "off." This is not because of a mistake you made but because you are awakening to a new perspective. Feeling off is a sign that your soul is sending you messages and pointing you toward new opportunities and potentials for your healing. As you perform these practices, try to release the outcome as well as your need to absolutely know and understand. Instead, call forth the courage to be wholly present within your second chakra feelings, a space rich with healing potential.

ESTABLISHING SAFETY
FOR EMOTIONAL HEALING

We cannot work with our feelings if we do not feel safe. This practice uses the safety established in the lower frequency of the root chakra and expands it as the foundation of your work with the sacral chakra.

Preparation

Sit quietly in a place that feels comfortable to you, perhaps placing your back against a wall or a tree. When your spine is sturdy, you're providing your nervous system with the feedback that nothing can sneak up behind you. This enables safety.

Intention

To create an energetic foundation of safety and security to support you in accessing your feelings and sacral energies.

Steps

» Rest your palms on your root chakra by placing your hands on either side of your hips.

» Through intention, connect with your first auric field, the one connected to your root chakra, which lies in the hips and governs safety and security. Your first auric field runs through your skin and all around your body.

» Offer the affirmation "I am safe" to your first chakra, and repeat that statement slowly three times or until you feel, sense, or experience a shift.

» As you notice yourself becoming more robust and grounded, move your hands onto your abdomen, infusing the second chakra with your affirmation and the associated energies of safety.

PRACTICE

BALANCING YOUR SECOND CHAKRA AND AURIC FIELD

Preparation

Find a quiet and welcoming space for this exercise. Bring paper and pen if you like to journal or process through writing. If you are a lover of color or art, gather paper and colored pencils.

Intention

To use your intuitive abilities for experiencing the qualities of your second chakra and associated auric field while using universal energies (energies available to all) to balance that chakra.

This practice is purely energetic; it isn't necessary to know why or understand the story behind the way this chakra is expressing. Instead, trust what you notice and that these universal energies support your balance.

Steps

» Sit or lie in any position that feels comfortable for you.

» Close your eyes or soften your gaze.

» Place your palms on your lower abdomen and, through intention, access your sacral chakra and its associated auric field, which surrounds the first chakra that runs through your skin. You might make a formal request, such as "I'd like to access my second chakra and auric field."

» Ask Creator or Spirit to bring forth universal energies to clear your second chakra and bring it into its most balanced expression. These energies will bring in new resources and remove unneeded energies. Remember, there may be a good reason your second chakra is not fully open and flowing. For example, when I was bullied as a child, it wasn't safe for me to fully open my feeling or sacral chakra. In my experience, if a chakra is presenting in a limited expression, when you use universal energies, compassion and love will flow and support a higher healing over time.

» Allow this balanced expression of your second chakra and auric field to integrate. You might take some notes, journal, or draw to help you process any shifts.

PRACTICE

THE LOTUS PETAL MEDITATION FOR CLEARING THE SACRAL CHAKRA

Sometimes healing isn't rooted in changing something but in acknowledging what is. Naming, witnessing, and acknowledging are other ways to work with your sacral chakra, as this feeling center allows you to process more deeply what is seen, felt, and experienced.

The trick is to allow what is to "be" without needing to change it. If you come to this practice honestly, fresh awareness will follow at the right time. As humans we find it hard to sit in the unknown, but I promise that if you stay with what's there, insights and healing will follow.

Consider an individual who is living with their romantic partner and struggling. You ask them to notice what happens when they come into the house: how they feel and what they see about their energy level, mood, and demeanor. They will probably report that their energy drops, that they feel their energy system contracting or tightening while their mood darkens. These signs reveal that the soul is restless. Then again, if a partnership is loving, the entry into the house will be heartening. Their energy level will heighten, and their feelings will be light.

Be as clear with yourself as you can be, using these steps as a guide.

Preparation

Create a quiet space and bring into it a pen and paper. As you approach this process, remember that your nervous system is hardwired to look for threats and discomforts. So don't be discouraged if the first energies to present themselves are tainted gray.

This inclination toward the negative is known as the negativity bias, and it comes from our earliest programming of scanning for threats. This constant searching helped keep humans safe when we lived with more immediate threats— like saber-toothed tigers! This is the reason that even now your body will first spy gloom or doom. Most often, your negativity bias will show up as fear, discomfort, sadness, or malaise. These are natural ways to create boundaries in your life. As the darker feelings arise, bring your healing witness to them. In this way, they will shift and make way for more positive perspectives and gentler emotions.

Intention

To help you name your feelings and be a healing witness to them.

Remember that your greatest healer is your inner and honest compassionate witness, who holds space for what is and releases the need to do anything immediately. Everything will shift in its right timing.

Steps

» On your paper, formulate a circle. This will be the center of a lotus or flower.

» While gazing at the circle, notice what you are feeling. Now create a petal off this center sphere and name that feeling within it. For example, this might be "sad," "confused," or "elated."

» Ask yourself, "What else am I feeling?" Draw another petal and write the name of that feeling in that space.

» Continue asking "What else?" while naming your feelings, creating a new petal for each.

» The lotus is said to have a thousand petals; continue to draw petals and name your feelings until you feel neutral. During this practice, you become your sacred healing witness. As you name these energies, many will mobilize and release. However, your sacral chakra will continue to hold on to some of them for as long as necessary, so be patient with yourself if a feeling doesn't budge for a while.

» Notice how much calmer and available you feel after this exercise.

PRACTICE

RESOURCING WITH AN ALLY

Another way to work with your second chakra is by resourcing with an ally, such as an angel, guide, parent, grandparent, friend, animal, your Higher Self, or even the Divine Mother or Father. I'll provide an example.

My client was in her mid-forties and had worked in corporate middle-tier management for many years. When she came to me, all she knew was that something felt "off" and she no longer felt like herself. I asked her to feel into that off-ness to see what emerged. Suddenly, she started coughing and said that her throat felt as though it was closing. She had a hard time speaking, although she was able to share that she seemed closed off from the world and quite small. She then continued to explore her awarenesses energetically.

These feelings led her into a childhood memory where she had felt unsafe and unprotected. She couldn't speak for herself. The energies of her fear and discomfort, along with the inability to speak, were locked together. The first step to her healing was to name the feelings connected to unmet needs. We called an energetic ally to support her and balanced her energy afterward.

By the end of our session, the feelings of contraction and off-ness had dissipated. Her energy was fully flowing and free. Three weeks later, she took a job with a new company and has been promoted twice over the last six months into an upper-level director position.

The power of our feelings is the root of our ability to create in our lives.

Preparation

Before beginning, take the time to name the feelings that may be lingering in your second chakra. Consider using the lotus practice above.

Intention

To bring an ally to help support the unmet need that is behind your feelings.

Steps

» Call forth the feeling or sensation from your sacral chakra.

» Ask yourself to see, sense, or know about the part of you who has been holding this feeling or sensation. Often this will be an aspect of you that wasn't originally seen, heard, acknowledged, or loved.

» Call on an ally to bring to you what you are missing. Perhaps a grandmother or an angel comes and holds the part of you that has been unseen or unappreciated. You will literally sense that they are embracing you.

» Allow the love to flow and occupy as much of your body as possible. It will most likely emanate from your sacral chakra to merge into the rest of your body.

» Ground yourself well after this practice. You can ground by taking a walk, spending a few minutes breathing deeply with bare feet on the earth or even your flooring, or participating in a favorite form of movement or exercise.

SUMMARY

The sacral chakra is the wellspring of your feelings and creative forces. The practices in this chapter will allow you to establish the sense of safety necessary for a deeper inquiry into the energies of this chakra. Using these practices will help you hear your soul, which shares through the language of feelings. You will become your own sacred witness and healing ally.

8

GUIDED MEDITATIONS

AMANDA HUGGINS

Meditating on the second or sacral chakra is a fantastic way to gracefully move through energetic seasons of "stuckness": periods of time where you're experiencing a sense of internal limitation. Stuckness can manifest in numerous ways, such as feeling creatively blocked, distanced from your inner sensuality, or weighed down by emotions.

While stuckness is rarely comfortable, it's usually sent as a signal from your sacral chakra, telling you that something within requires balancing, nurturing, or tending to.

I like to explore sacral chakra work in two primary ways: witnessing and welcoming. By moving into the resistance and tuning in to your second chakra, you will have the opportunity to release your stuckness and reclaim your divine creative ability to express.

The act of witnessing the emotions, memories, and resistance stored in your sacral chakra creates space to welcome more creativity, pleasure, and playfulness. Bringing the second chakra into balance is a continued practice in release and replenishment, one that ultimately can bring both healing and pleasure in equal measure.

It's not always obvious what emotions and energy we've been holding on to within our sacral chakra. Living in today's fast-paced society, it's only natural that we'll pick up emotions and forget to process or put them back down again. And sometimes the energy we've picked up isn't even ours! When we're able to engage in a curious, nonjudgmental practice of witnessing our energy and emotions, we can then begin to safely release what no longer serves us (or was never ours to begin with).

Release, of course, means that we now have lots of wonderful new energetic space to fill back up. This is the fun, pleasurable work of the second chakra: granting ourselves permission to express our thoughts, emotions, and creativity. The more we can invoke a sense of joy, pleasure, or playfulness in our lives, the easier (and more enjoyable) it becomes to bring the second chakra back into balance.

MEDITATING AND CONNECTING
WITH THE SACRAL CHAKRA

Each of the three meditations in this chapter offers a slightly different access point for connecting with your sacral chakra.

The first meditation is a simple color-based visualization. You'll have the opportunity to connect with and explore your second chakra and allow your intuition to inform and perform any energetic tune-ups you need.

The second meditation serves as an opportunity to witness and honor any emotions or energy that may be stored in your second chakra. You'll be encouraged to engage in curious, spacious, and compassionate dialogue with your second chakra, and create space to begin mindfully releasing what you no longer need.

The third meditation is a more playful—and more active—practice. Rather than going through a traditional stationary meditation, you'll have the chance to explore meditation through movement and grant yourself permission to explore pleasurable, playful, creative expression.

In both meditation and life at large, my personal philosophy is to take what you need and leave the rest. Any elements of the following meditations can be combined or altered based on your own intuitive guidance. Take what you need and allow the wisdom of your own energy centers to expand upon the rest. Creative expression is central to the second chakra, after all!

PRACTICE

COLOR-BASED VISUALIZATION FOR SACRAL HEALING

Find a comfortable meditation position. I suggest lying down, allowing your entire body to relax. It may feel nice to find a supported *supta baddha konasana* (reclined butterfly pose), using a pillow under each knee for support.

Draw one hand to the low belly and one hand to the heart with palms facing down, connected to the body.

Take a few breaths to still the body as you allow your eyes to close. Gently scan your body from head to toe, searching for any spaces that are holding tension or resistance. Pay attention to your shoulders, jaw, and especially hips and lower belly area where the sacral chakra resides. Let go of any restriction or tension in the low belly, allowing it to be soft and unrestricted.

Take a cleansing breath in and then breathe out any residual tension in the body. Allow the breath to fall into a natural and soothing cadence.

Place your attention on your hips and low belly area, and draw your focus inward toward the center of the sacral chakra. Begin to visualize a beautiful orange light swirling around in a counterclockwise motion. Simply gaze at the chakra and witness this.

Notice the size, shape, vibrancy, and texture of the chakra. See if you're able to gain an understanding of how it's working. Does it feel like it's moving quickly or slowly? Is the light vibrant or dull? How much space does the light of this chakra take up? Notice without judgment.

As you continue to breathe, allow your intuitive guidance to adjust the orange light. Perhaps you'd like to turn the brightness, speed, or vibration up or down. Maybe you're drawn to play with the warmth, depth, or intensity of the light. Watch as the glow of the orange chakra begins to morph into your optimal level of vibrancy and vibration.

Continue to breathe and allow that orange light to expand from your sacral chakra and move outward in all directions. Watch as the light envelops your body, and notice how far the light of your chakra travels. Breathe and receive this energy.

Continue to breathe within this beautiful dome of orange light. Use the exhalations to let go of any tension or emotional resistance that arise.

Allow your inhalations to fill those spaces of surrender back up with feelings of joy, trust, and creativity. Enjoy the space and breathe here if you'd like.

When you're ready to close the meditation, draw the orange light inward and into the sacral chakra.

Bring your awareness back to the cadence of your breath. Gently deepen the breath, drawing your energy and awareness back into your body and the room around you.

When you're ready, blink your eyes open and return to your surroundings.

PRACTICE

THE WITNESSING AND HONORING MEDITATION

This meditation allows you to witness the emotions and energies that have made a home in your sacral chakra. Through your breath and intuition, you can witness the emotions or experiences you're holding on to and release whatever you choose to.

Get comfortable, either sitting or lying down.

Place both hands on the lower belly. Feel the warmth of your palms penetrating through the layers of skin, muscle, and tissue, and connect directly with your sacral chakra.

Take a few minutes to find ease within this connection. Breathe deeply, and allow the body to relax into feelings of trust, comfort, and warmth.

If you notice any tension arising in your body, simply breathe into that space. When you find resistance in your mind, practice forgiveness and draw your attention back to the breath. Simply place all your awareness within your second chakra.

Hold your awareness in this space as you offer yourself a gentle, loving reminder: *I am here to witness, to love, and to release. I am here for me.*

Invite a spirit of inquiry into your body and mind as you begin to engage in curious, openhearted inquiry through a series of reflective questions. For each of the reflections, simply allow any awarenesses or responses to come up. This is much less a practice in thinking or doing and much more a practice in witnessing and receiving. Notice when the lizard brain tries to take hold and pull you away from receiving or witnessing. Continue reconnecting to the wisdom of your sacral space over and over again.

You may use the following inquiry prompts to witness, explore, and release as you see fit. Allow the intuitive guidance of your second chakra to alter or expand on any of these inquiries and to direct when it's time to move into the next reflection.

Inquiry Prompts

» What unprocessed emotions or energetic residue are taking up space within this chakra?

» What feelings are asking me to witness them?

> *Open space to witness, honor, and*
> *feel the feelings that come up.*

» Are these emotions and energy mine? If not, whose energy are they? Who else are they connected to and why?

» What can I do to safely begin releasing what no longer serves me?

> *Use your breath—specifically, your*
> *exhalations—to create energetic release.*
> *You may stay here as long as you'd like.*

» How can I offer more comfort and emotional safety to this energy center?

» Is there anything else my sacral space would like to communicate to me?

When you feel complete, you may close the meditation by deepening your breath and bringing your awareness back into the body. Gently open your eyes again.

It's important to note that, depending on your personal experiences, this level of meditative inquiry may feel quite deep or even intense. You may experience a wave of insight, a swell of emotions, or perhaps even receive an important new awareness about yourself. It's always a good idea to have a journal handy to capture any insights that come through—and perhaps a box of tissues to wipe away any tears that come up as a byproduct of any release.

PRACTICE

PLEASURE AND CREATIVITY ACTIVATION: A MOVING MEDITATION

This meditation is slightly more active than a traditional seated meditation practice. Movement is an incredibly powerful way to release stuckness and reconnect to emotional and creative expression, and this meditation will offer space to access your own expression in a fun yet meditative way.

In this practice you'll access your body's own intuitive and creative wisdom to mindfully move in ways that feel good. You'll give yourself permission to play while accessing feelings of pleasure and creativity.

First, you'll want to set your environment. Choose a room that has ample space for you to move in. Make sure the floor is free of clutter and there are no hard corners that you might bang into. Once you've assured that you have a safe and comfortable space, it's time to set the tone with sound.

Select a few songs that have consistent, rhythmic beats—something you immediately connect to and want to move to. This doesn't necessarily have to be traditional yoga or meditation music; you might want to select some songs from one of your favorite artists or find a rhythmic playlist that makes your body want to move. The intention is to choose sounds that call you forward and elicit a desire to surrender into the beat or pace of the music.

Once you've selected your songs—and made sure you've got some comfy clothes to move in—turn your playlist on and stand in the center of your room.

Allow your eyes to close, and place both hands on the low belly to connect with your sacral chakra. Spend the first few moments breathing deeply as you focus your energy within the sacral space.

Begin to breathe through the sacral chakra, syncing your inhalations and exhalations with the rhythm of the music.

Remain still at first as you simply allow your inner rhythm to build and move throughout your entire body.

As you feel the pulse of your sacral chakra, allow your body's stillness to shift into intuitive, free-form movement. Let your body move exactly how it wants to, exactly in ways that feel good. Move with the breath and allow your creative expression to work through your body.

Notice how good it feels to truly allow yourself to let go, express, and allow your body to be in communion with the frequency of sound. Bask in feelings of joy and pleasure as you move, shake, release, and express.

This isn't about looking cool or hitting dance moves the right way; it's a practice in allowing the body to experience pleasure through judgment-free, creative movement.

Your movements can be as wild, bold, sensual, or loud as you want. Do what feels good! Trust your body; trust your sacral chakra. Use this practice as pure expression. Your breath, body, and sacral chakra will guide you.

I want to note that while this is designed to be a fun, spacious, expressive practice, it's totally normal if it feels uncomfortable at first! For many of us, it's foreign to dance or move or express with full abandon. If you notice you're feeling resistance or self-judgment, simplify and reconnect with your meditative breath. Let the energy rebuild, then start to move again.

You may feel complete after just two or three songs. When your body tells you it's time to finish the practice, bring your body back into stillness. Once more, place both hands on top of your sacral space and breathe deeply.

As you close your practice, repeat the following before opening your eyes:

9

VIBRATIONAL REMEDIES

JO-ANNE BROWN

When I ponder the power of vibrational remedies to support the sacral chakra, I am reminded of a young client I worked with many years ago.

He was a quiet, shy boy who suffered from bed-wetting, increasing deafness, fatigue, and digestive issues. His parents had been told he would need surgery to resolve his hearing problems. Discovering he had a high toxic load from bacteria, viruses, molds, and heavy metals, I treated him with vibrational remedies and therapies.

I started by unburdening his young system of the microbial overload and toxins, focusing first on bacteria (urinary system) and mold (ears). I also introduced frequencies to further support his body's natural detoxification processes.

After just one session, his urinary control, hearing, and energy levels greatly improved, and his other symptoms lessened.

His life had been transformed in just sixty minutes by vibrational remedies that stimulated and enabled his healthy second chakra energies.

Vibrational remedies are not only supportive of children. They support all of us as we embody and embrace healthy second chakra energies, both physical and subtle.

In this chapter, I will increase your awareness of how vibrational remedies support and empower the second chakra by:

> » explaining what they are
>
> » describing how they benefit us
>
> » examining the difference between support-based and tangible remedies
>
> » sharing specific second chakra–supporting remedies with you
>
> » providing you with two practices to support your second chakra at home

WHAT ARE VIBRATIONAL REMEDIES?

Vibrational remedies hold energies that are inherently harmonizing. This means that when they enter a disruptive and chaotic environment, these remedies have the capacity to restore it to harmony and balance.

For the sacral chakra and its bodily systems, balance and harmony occur when flow and healthy movement are achieved.

We have learned that the sacral chakra represents emotional energy, feelings, intuition, empathy, and other subtle aspects. While our root chakra, located near the hips, enables survival, the sacral chakra brings us into a state of thriving. It relates to the emotions and feelings derived from a family or tribal context rather than the singularity of the root chakra.

The second chakra is coded with knowledge of which emotions and feelings are acceptable—and unacceptable—to our tribe. We are also influenced by our ancestors' experiences through genetic patterning. And we embody all our learnings within our emotional second chakra center in the form of values, belief systems, thoughts, and behaviors.

WHAT IS RESONANCE?

Vibrational remedies are subject to a phenomenon called resonance.

Resonance is what happens when one object responds (or vibrates) at the same natural frequency as a secondary object. There are examples of resonance all around us. We see resonance in a children's park when a child is on a swing.

The person pushing the swing must sync, or resonate, with the motion of the swing. If the pushing of the swing is out of sync with the swing's motion, the flow is interrupted and dissonance—the opposite of resonance—results.

With vibrational remedies, resonance is achieved when the intended results of a remedy are realized within a person.

Second chakra remedies work for us in one of two ways. They either remind us of our existing second chakra strengths or they introduce us to positive second chakra qualities we are not already expressing.

THE ROLE OF WATER
IN VIBRATIONAL REMEDIES

Liquid-based vibrational remedies are typically created from three primary components: a carrier solution, a preserving agent, and the core vibrational essence of the remedy.

The most common carrier solution in vibrational remedies is water. This is not just due to its ready availability. The water molecule (H_2O) contains remarkable and unique properties that allow it to both store and carry information as well as influence how our personal biomolecules interact (including our DNA, hormones, neurotransmitters, and amino acids).

The water molecule consists of two positively charged hydrogen atoms bonded with one negatively charged oxygen atom. This positive and negative polarity enables a unique form of bonding between molecules that allows the easy formation of large water clusters, which have 280 or more molecules. These clusters naturally form into a network that resembles a twenty-sided platonic solid with triangular faces, the icosahedron.

These large water clusters also increase the storage capacity of water and its ability to remember vast amounts of vibrational information.

We already know the sacral chakra rules the body's reproductive system, genitourinary system, and enteric nervous system, which regulates the movement of water and electrolytes. Notice that these systems are all about movement and flow.

Dehydration in these second chakra systems can have dire consequences, including long-term damage (urinary system), compromised genetic viability (eggs and sperm), and increased stress (enteric nervous system).

Remember, the average human adult body is 60 percent water. Water is required in every cell of our body, not only for our survival but so we can flourish and thrive.

And when our bodies are well hydrated, the essences carried by water clusters in vibrational remedies are easily able to reach their intended destinations.

VIBRATIONAL REMEDIES FOR OUR SECOND CHAKRA

Vibrational remedies fall into one of two categories:

> » support-based remedies
>
> » tangible remedies

Support-Based Vibrational Remedies

Support-based vibrational remedies include treatments, therapies, and practices that work with subtle energies. They often require the presence and guidance of a healing practitioner and support our water-moon chakra energies through

> » skin-to-skin contact, including acupressure, acupuncture, kinesiology, massage, reflexology, and therapeutic touch techniques
>
> » vibrational media, including color/crystal/ chakra therapies, frequency-based modalities, sound/vocal therapy, Reiki, and toning
>
> » demonstrational guidance, including yoga and Emotional Freedom Technique (EFT tapping)
>
> » immersive therapies

I believe skin-to-skin contact remedies are best experienced personally because their benefits can vary greatly.

I will now highlight three modalities in greater detail, as I find them extremely effective for second chakra embodiment. They are also easily accessible, with or without a practitioner.

Two of these methods are vibrational media—sound therapies and frequency-based modalities—and the third modality, floatation therapy, sits in the immersive therapy category.

SOUND THERAPIES. In traditional Chinese medicine (TCM), the sense organs for the kidneys are the ears. For this reason, I strongly encourage the use of sound therapies for sacral chakra empowerment.

One of my favorite tools for shifting stuck second chakra energies is the rain stick, which has been used for centuries by indigenous communities to summon elemental water energy in the form of rain.

I also use music based on the solfeggio frequencies (285, 417, 528, and 852 Hz) that align with the soul or spiritual plane (from numerology) to support the sacral chakra. The

285 Hz frequency induces a state of conscious calm, while the 417 Hz, along with the 528 Hz frequency, activates creativity and intuition. The 528 Hz frequency also resonates beautifully with water-based remedies and therapies. The 852 Hz frequency helps us connect to our intuitive powers and spiritual guidance.

FREQUENCY-BASED THERAPIES. These therapies use low voltage frequency–generating devices such as the Rife machine to send selected therapeutic vibrations to the body, typically through conductive electrodes.

When received by the body during a therapy session, these vibrations easily effect positive change in the second chakra organ systems.

For example, blocked kidney meridian energy can be released using the 60 Hz and 127 kHz frequencies. If possible, it is ideal to apply conductive electrodes to the soles of the feet to directly influence the kidney meridian at its starting point, Kidney-1, also called Bubbling Spring in TCM.

FLOATATION THERAPY. This therapy takes place in a low-stimulation floatation chamber that contains warm water infused with high concentrations of magnesium sulfate, or Epsom salts.

This potent sacral chakra remedy provides long-lasting relief from inflammatory conditions and supports the vagus nerve, a vital enteric nervous system component, by restoring its ability to shift from a stressed sympathetic state back to a more relaxed parasympathetic state.

Tangible Vibrational Remedies

Tangible remedies are literally "medicines" and have a distinct advantage over support-based remedies because they are portable. These remedies are received into the body orally via drops and pills, through diffusion methods via essential oils, and through the skin via oils, ointments, and salves. They include homeopathic remedies, flower essences, and essential oils.

Infused remedies intrinsically support us through their presence in our immediate environment. These are a subcategory of tangible remedies that include crystals, jewelry, and amulets.

HOMEOPATHIC REMEDIES. Homeopathy is a system of resonance-based medicine based on the law of similars, in which the substance that triggers disease or dysfunction is used to treat that same disease or dysfunction.

During diagnosis, practitioners prescribe a suitable remedy of an appropriate potency to invoke a healing response in the patient.

These remedies support our emotional second chakra landscape and are best treated using lower-potency remedies, starting from lowest to highest, in the range of 30C and 200C dosages.

Homeopathic remedies that promote healthy second chakra energies include Agnus Castus, Cantharis, Mag Phos, Pulsatilla, Sepia, Spigelia anthelmia, Staphysagria, and Thuja.

FLOWER ESSENCES. The earliest known use of flower essences, as recorded on papyrus, was by ancient Egyptians who collected the dew of flowers to treat emotional problems more than three thousand years ago.

While there are many ranges of flower essences available, I'm featuring Australian Bush Flower Essences and Flower Essence Services Quintessentials essences because I've personally experienced and seen their empowering qualities at work.

» *Australian Bush Flower Essences:* This range of flower-based remedies was formulated by Australian Ian White to balance and harmonize our well-being by supporting our subtle energies. Ian comes from a long line of herbalists, beginning with his great-grandmother, who worked as an herbalist during Australia's Gold Rush in the 1850s. Australian Bush Flower remedies for the second chakra include Creative Essence (for creative expression), Sexuality Essence (for sexual intimacy), Flannel Flower (for emotional intimacy), Little Flannel Flower (for joy and childlike wonder), She Oak (for hormonal balance and rehydration), Turkey Bush (for enhanced creativity), and the Water Essence remedy from the White Light range (for emotional harmony).

» *Flower Essence Services Quintessentials essences:* The 103 individual flower essences in this range are liquid potentized extracts derived from flowers grown in pristine wildflower habitats in the US. These remedies were developed to resolve stuck or unbalanced emotional aspects of mind-body wellness. I have found the most beneficial second chakra remedies in this range include Evening Primrose (for healthy emotional connection), Sticky Monkeyflower (for loving sexual connection), and Yerba Santa (for healthy emotional expression).

Here are two vibrational practices to support your second chakra.

PRACTICE

RECEIVE A SECOND CHAKRA
ATTRIBUTE THROUGH SACRED GEOMETRY

The icosahedron is a sacred geometry form, a platonic solid that is beautifully aligned with water and, by extension, the water-moon chakra.

This practice can be done visually or through direct contact with an icosahedron. You can either visualize an icosahedron in your mind's eye, look at an image of it, or hold a solid icosahedron in your left hand.

If you wish to work energetically with platonic solid geometry moving forward, you may choose to purchase a solid set, such as one made from crystal, wood, or glass.

Would you like to more fully embody a specific second chakra attribute or quality? Start by selecting one of the following attributes: sensitivity, creativity, compassion, intuition, sensuality, or empathy.

Now turn your attention to the icosahedron.

As you do this, focus on its external structure. Bring your awareness to the incredible ability of water molecules to bond, forming icosahedral clusters or networks. Consider the truth that personalized vibrational messages are contained deep within these clusters. As you redirect your attention within the icosahedron, picture your chosen attribute at the very center. It is a special package of vibrational energy just for you and is exactly what you asked for. Visualize your chosen attribute moving slowly from the center of the icosahedron into your second chakra. As you willingly receive the attribute, you may sense a beautiful orange glow as it is lovingly activated within your sacral chakra.

PRACTICE

USE REMEDIES TO FIND
BALANCE IN YOUR RELATIONSHIPS

Are you experiencing strong emotions around your relationship with a loved one? When your sacral chakra needs support, you can have trouble finding balance in your relationships.

This simple practice will provide you with emotional support as you find a place for both the relationship itself and for you within the relationship.

You will need a glass of water, preferably filtered, and either a sprinkle of Epsom salts or a second chakra flower essence remedy. Several recommended remedies are listed on page 143.

» Place the glass of filtered water in front of you.

» Either sprinkle the Epsom salts into the water and stir or add the recommended dosage (in drops) of the flower essence.

» Before you drink the infused water, express gratitude to your second chakra for its role in holding and bringing to your attention your emotional needs.

» Drink the infused water at your own pace.

» If you are working with a flower essence, you will benefit from repeating this practice either daily or twice daily, depending on the recommended dosage.

SUMMARY

Vibrational remedies are created to move, unblock, or balance our second chakra energies. When we embrace the power of second chakra remedies, we enable a healthy shift from a first chakra focus on physical survival to a second chakra focus on ease, flow, and pleasure.

We sometimes forget that emotions and feelings convey powerful vibrational messages. But through its watery connections, our sacral chakra influences us in body, mind, and spirit.

This chapter has shared therapies, remedies, and practices that enhance our embodiment of powerful sacral chakra attributes. Now that you've learned about them, I encourage you to experience their benefits firsthand!

10

CRYSTALS, MINERALS, AND STONES

MARGARET ANN LEMBO

Your creative life force is located at the second chakra, just below your belly button. Your ability to give birth is located at this center. Whether you are giving birth to a child, a book, a new business, or a piece of artwork, the energy of creation is derived from the sacral chakra. This is the center that holds the energy of fertility. You can be fertile with ideas just as you can be fertile for childbirth. The energy to manifest comes from this chakra, and you can use crystals, minerals, and stones to help accomplish all manifestations.

DIRECT WITH INTENTION

To enable a dream to come true with your water-moon chakra energies, start by organizing your thoughts. Make a list of what you want. Arrange these thoughts into categories of goals such as income, career, family, travel, physical, social, educational, and spiritual. Written intentions clarify and crystallize your objective. Prioritize, visualize, make lists, and set deadlines. Establishing a deadline creates a chemical reaction in your body, mind, and spirit to make the goal a reality.

When a gemstone is paired with a daily affirmation, the stone amplifies and helps maintain focus on that intention. In my work with color and crystals over the course of over three decades, I've found that to use a stone most effectively, it is best to associate an intention with it.

It's easy to choose the perfect stone to match your intention. Simply focus on the image or thought of your intention and then look at the choices of crystals available to you, either in a store or in your own private collection. I'll provide my recommendations on which stones to use, but trust your own inner guidance. If you are attracted to a stone while you are choosing gems, go with your gut and what is attractive to you. Match your positive thought with that gemstone, and watch your world realign with what you decide you want to create.

BALANCED EMOTIONS

Emotions can get stuck in the sacral chakra, especially the remnants of mental, physical, and verbal abuse. Sometimes people who have experienced abuse have digestive problems. The sacral chakra is physically located at the place where the biological function of elimination occurs. Look at digestion from a metaphysical standpoint to see what thoughts, feelings, and emotions must be eliminated to let new, positive, empowering experiences into your life.

Use complementary colors to restore equilibrium. Remember the color chart you learned as a child? You can use the colors that are opposite the color of a given chakra, selecting a stone with that hue.

Notice that some of the stones listed below aren't orange, the main color associated with the sacral chakra. You can use any number of stones for sacral balancing because it's about frequencies—the frequencies needed to clear emotions, restore emotional stability, and innovate your dreams into coming true.

My favorite gemstones for emotional balancing and creative inspiration are as follows:

Lepidolite carries the vibration of lithium, which is used medically to balance the emotions. This stone is beneficial for depression and mental illness stemming from mood swings. Decide that it is time to restore well-being. A joyful outlook on life can be yours. Take the necessary steps to shift your focus from troubling thoughts to those that bring you joy. Recognize that life flows in circles, and all cycles shift and change. Focus on how you want your reality to manifest. Employ affirmations like these: *I embrace my* *emotions. Nurturing energy surrounds me. My emotional body is aligned. I am calm. I am serene. Tranquility and peace are mine.*

Orange calcite helps you process feelings that have been stored in your consciousness for a long time. Calcite's gentle orange vibration helps you release stuck emotions with a gentle push. This is the perfect stone to install positive thoughtforms, or mental energy, in the emotional body immediately after an emotional release. Orange calcite entices you to use your creativity, which encourages action and play and fosters a fertile life. Use an affirmation like these: *I embrace change. I have creative ideas that I easily bring into reality. I trust in the day's relaxed flow.*

CREATIVITY AND FERTILITY

Your second chakra is a wellspring of innovation and fertility, the latter being the energy of growth. What stones can you use for these purposes?

Carnelian, an orange or red form of chalcedony, is best used as a catalyst to put things in motion so they can come to fruition. I keep a carnelian on my writing desk as a tool to keep writing and finish manuscripts. This is also one of the best gems for those who want a fertility amulet as they prepare to become parents. Carnelian is great to help you dive into your emotions through art, music, writing, or any creative outlet. This stone also helps you embrace the emotions and feelings of past challenges, accept them, and move on. A stone for action and moving forward in life, it is useful when you are up against an emotional block. With good visualization and trust in your imagination, think good thoughts like these: *I am fertile in body, mind, and spirit. Creativity flows through me in myriad ways. I am courageous and bravely bring my ideas into actuality. My imagination is the key to my success. I envision my future and joyfully participate as it unfolds.*

Blue topaz, also associated with the throat chakra, brings inspiration to artists, authors, inventors, or anyone who is creating something, whether it is a garden or a meal. As a stone of creative inspiration, it is useful for overcoming writer's block. Use the clear blue of this gemstone to open your channel to bring ideas in through you and then move them into manifest reality through clear actions. It is time to allow your inner artist to step forward. Thoughts like these can aid in bringing the creative energy through you: *I have great ideas all the time. My creative juices are flowing. My mind is clear and bright. I communicate well. I always find the right words when speaking or writing, and people listen to me.*

CUTTING THE
CORDS OF THE PAST

Etheric cords of attachment to people and events are often stuck in the energy field. You are linked to every person you have ever interacted with, regardless of whether you are consciously aware of it. The attachments coming from past relationships may carry the vibration of jealousy or some other negativity, causing sacral issues. You can also absorb others' feelings through these energetic cords.

Such cords can drain your energy, weaken your vibrancy, and even lower your self-esteem. Your attachments may be to the past rather than to an actual person. Events that hurt you emotionally, mentally, and physically replay in your mind repeatedly, sometimes consciously and sometimes unconsciously. These types of attachments can also prevent you from living your life to the fullest.

Use visualization and the following gems to disengage all cords of attachment that aren't for your highest good. I've included a visualization practice at the end of this section to help you do just that. Basically, you can incorporate these gems into your life to seal any openings in your auric field or release the cords that could be holding you back.

Black obsidian arrowhead uses the shape of an arrow as a reminder that there are always signs pointing you in the right direction. This volcanic black glass—especially when shaped into an arrowhead—reminds you to use your visualization skills to cut the cords that are attached to past relationships. You can use black obsidian in a sphere or palm stone shape as a tool for looking within to the source of emotional challenges. Use it to help with self-observation and improve situational awareness. Use these affirmations: *I am responsible for my happiness. I release the cords that bind me. I stay with matters until they are settled or reach completion. I pay attention to what is going on around me and within me. I am attentive.*

Smoky quartz is a brown to black variety of quartz. When used with conscious intent, it can cauterize emotional wounds. Therefore, this is a perfect crystal to work with when you are cutting a cord of the past. I have found smoky quartz especially beneficial when I want to release emotionally charged thoughts and feelings. Good for dealing with emotions, use smoky quartz to seal and heal buried wounds on a vibrational level. The place where the cords are attached in the energy body creates an energetic hole. When used with conscious intent, smoky quartz grounds, protects, and seals the energetic hole. Believe yourself when you repeat these types of affirmations: *I am divinely protected. I easily refocus my efforts away from distractions. I honor my grounded connection with Mother Earth.*

PRACTICE

RELEASING SACRAL CORDS BY VISUALIZING ETHERIC GEMSTONES

If subtle energies are real but not concrete, the same could be said of the energy of gemstones. As we saw in the last discussion about the need to let go of cords or energetic attachments that cause negativity, specific gemstones can empower those efforts. Why not access our innate ability to visualize processes and outcomes and mix it with our capability for calling up the energy of (or spirits connected to) gemstones?

I'm going to walk you through a practice that will help you check for invisible attachments causing sacral challenges. I'll then have you select one of the featured release-oriented gemstones—black obsidian arrowhead, black tourmaline or tourmalinated quartz, or smoky quartz—to free yourself from a feeling, person, situation, or even negative entity or energy blocking your sacral chakra. You can use this same exercise for any reason with stones you can hold in your hand or your imagination.

Find a space where you won't be disturbed for a few minutes. Take a full breath and put one or both hands on your abdomen. Inhale deeply enough that you feel your abdomen rise, and then exhale completely and feel it fall. Now request that your own inner spirit or the Divine help you attune to your sacral chakra.

Place your consciousness in the middle of this orange center of swirling love and emotion. Then request that guidance help you intuitively sense, feel, see, hear, or became aware of a cord or subtle attachment that might be limiting the full effectiveness of your water-moon chakra. If there is such a presence, ask that your inner sage or an external spirit guide help you comprehend its origin and impact.

Is this attachment linked to a person or perhaps an event or situation? Does this object relate to the past, present, or a dream or fear about the future? Sometimes we hold on to animals, deceased ancestors, or even supernatural figures.

Let yourself sense how this attachment is influencing you, and when you're ready, visualize which of these stones seems most powerful for the purpose of releasing the cord:

» Black obsidian arrowhead is particularly helpful when releasing cords and regaining independence.

» Black tourmaline or tourmalinated quartz is good at purifying your own energy while deflecting negativity.

» Use smoky quartz to bandage and heal past wounds.

Whichever stone makes its way into your mind, imagine that you are holding it in your hand over your abdomen. Its energy releases like a cloud and enters your sacral chakra, clearing out the negativity and healing any emotional, relationship, psychic, or other injuries. Any cords are automatically disintegrated. The black or gray smoke emanating from the stone turns white and then orange, filling in your sacral chakra with cheer and goodwill. When you feel complete, let go of this process, put your pretend stone away for the time being, and reengage with your life.

DREAMING

In many cultures, the sacral chakra is considered a place of power, a dreaming center, and a focus point for manifestation. It is said that what manifests is first created in the dreamtime. Dreaming can also be prophetic, preparing you for what is to come or alerting you to fulfill your life's purpose. The sacral chakra is an energy center where intuition dwells. You have probably heard the expression "Go with your gut feeling," which stems from the knowledge that your feelings of intuition are physically located in the band of energy at the navel region. There are several crystals that help amplify dreams, dreaming, and dream recall. Here are a few to help you along the way:

Amethyst, or purple quartz, comes in many forms, including chevron-banded amethyst, cactus quartz, amethyst clusters, and ametrine (amethyst and citrine together in the same stone). Amethyst is an excellent stone for dreaming, dream interpretation, and encouraging pleasant dreams. Amethyst is well known to stimulate the intuition. Use it to tap into deeper levels of your consciousness that you access during the dreamtime. Make it your intention to remember your dreams, and repeat something like this before you fall asleep: *I use my intuition and follow my hunches. I pay attention to my dreams and interpret their messages easily.*

Moonstone, with its innate ability to activate extraordinary awareness, is a perfect tool for increasing your intuition and trusting the process of becoming an intuitive. Moonstone promotes dreaming. Dreams provide tools for self-knowledge and help bring mental clarity. With moonstone under your pillow, use the messages of the dreamtime to restore mental balance. State these phrases with the clear intention to recall your dreams: *I am extremely intuitive and perceptive. I awaken my consciousness and become aware of my dreams and the messages within my dreams.*

11

MANTRA HEALING

TIA TUENGE

Mantras offer the amazing ability to bring balance to your second chakra, known in the West as the sacral or hara chakra. The word *hara* references the belly, and that's exactly where your water-moon chakra lies.

Associated with creativity, birthing, and bringing forth, your second chakra is linked to sensuality and the waxing and waning of energy. Who doesn't yearn for healthy emotions and the ability to link with the manifesting and divine feminine power of this chakra? When we're operating from this womb or hara space, we're able to create the lives we envision. Given that this is a water chakra, it is especially conducive to sound and the formation of mantras that enable prosperity and joy.

In this chapter I'll unpack the idea of utilizing mantras to enable all things second chakra. I'll explain what mantras are, how they work, and how to compose powerful mantras that will support a vivid second chakra and the expression it invites for yourself and others.

WHAT IS A MANTRA?

Let's start at the beginning with an exploration of mantras and how they benefit the sacral chakra.

The word *mantra* derives from Vedic Sanskrit and relates to a sacred word, sound, or phrase. It is a holy sound, a whisper of love. *Man* means to think or mind, and *tra* means tool. Add these terms together and you have defined a mantra: a tool used to guide and focus the mind.

Some experts suggest you mainly use traditional mantras, which have been sculpted across time. These are typically pulled from Vedic Sanskrit phrases, although there are many branches of yoga that offer their own formulated phrases that are believed to link directly to the Divine. There are personal mantras too, which can also be called affirmations.

Why do some individuals assert that you should only use the ancient sacred Sanskrit phrases? They contain special vibrational frequencies, as well as the energy and intentions of the millions of people who have recited them over millennia. Why not draw from this pool of wisdom? In this school, it is thought that affirmations do not contain these benefits. Yet I know from my own experience, and from the work I do with clients, that there is great power in creating personal mantras that are targeted to a specific feeling and outcome.

In this chapter I'll cover both traditional Sanskrit mantras and powerful personal mantras designed to bring about meaningful transformation. As to which to choose—and I suggest you try both—there are as many options for choosing a mantra as there are people. You get to decide what feels right for you based on the process you desire and the outcome you intend. Whatever your choice, the key is to be willing to repeat a mantra again and again, inviting it to become a part of your body, mind, and soul.

CREATING AND USING PERSONAL MANTRAS

There is an art and science to creating your own personal mantras. The art is in identifying what needs healing. The science involves formulating a mantra that specifically targets the area or issue you desire to heal. Let's explore how to pinpoint what may not be working by clarifying what an optimally healthy sacral chakra is and is not.

When our sacral chakra is healthy, we feel creative and capable. We are emotionally balanced and comfortable with intimacy. We give way to the flow of life and recognize the many marvelous synchronicities on the riverway we're part of. When our second chakra is out of balance, however, we might feel stuck and unable to move forward. Our emotional wounds are oh so obvious, and we're easily overwhelmed. We might also experience difficulties with sexual intimacy or loving our own bodies.

I once worked with a client who had a classic sacral chakra block. She had gone through a painful divorce years before and felt ready to meet someone new. She desired a meaningful relationship but couldn't seem to meet anyone.

There were layers to her blocks. For one, she was stuck in a time-consuming job that she didn't like, yet she seemed unable to forge a new career opportunity. In turn, her time commitments made it almost impossible to explore the dating world. Once she did the root chakra work to feel safe and secure, which are the keystones of the first chakra, we designed a plan to heal her sacral chakra. And guess what? She met someone! (I'll clue you in to what she did at various points in the rest of this chapter.)

When the sacral chakra is healthy and vibrant, we feel joyous, creative, sexy, energized, and empowered. If you're not enjoying those qualities, the following exercises will help you identify where you're currently at and what your soul desires. These practices culminate in forming mantras that will enhance a healthy second chakra.

FORMULATING A MANTRA, STEP 1: INNER EXPLORATION

Prepare to create your own empowering mantras by making time for an inner adventure. Simply respond to these journaling prompts:

> » How am I feeling right now?
>
> » How do I want to feel?
>
> » Three activities that bring me joy are . . .
>
> » Three events that give me energy are . . .
>
> » Three goals I want to experience in the next three months are . . .
>
> » Gifts I will give myself in the next three months include . . .

Spend as much time as needed to answer these questions while getting to know yourself on a deeper level.

FORMULATING A MANTRA, STEP 2: MAKING A YES MAP

A yes map is a fun and easy way to get your creative juices flowing while specifically identifying what you'd like to create in your life. For this step, simply write down everything you want to say yes to on one page of your journal or on a piece of paper.

In the case of my client, she decided that she would say yes to making time outside work for the activities that brought her joy. She saw this as a crucial stage for eventually saying yes to an intimate, mutually supportive relationship. By committing to her personal passions, she opened her second chakra to relationship passion. She then used the journaling prompts and her yes map to craft personal mantras that energized and affirmed her ideal life, as you'll be doing in the next step.

PRACTICE

FORMULATING A MANTRA, STEP 3: TURNING YESES INTO MANTRAS

Based on your yeses, it's now time to sculpt your mantras. All you must do is take a yes and put the meaning of it into a simple statement. For instance, if you want to say yes to romantic love, you can fashion a mantra like *I am now enjoying a fully satisfying romantic partnership.*

The following constitute versions of the personal mantras that the client I've been discussing fashioned as well as mantras that other clients have created over the years. The only rule is to make mantras that zing and sing for you— mantras you can feel deep inside your sacral chakra and are excited to bring to life! Remember that sacral chakra mantras will assist you with desires like living joyfully, opening up emotionally, allowing for trust and intimacy, and getting into the creative flow. Keep in mind that an effective personal mantra is written in the present tense and stated positively.

Here are some sample second chakra mantras:

- » I allow myself to be fully creative.
- » Innovative energy flows through me freely.
- » I am an expressive being.
- » I feel joyful, energetic, and alive.
- » I fully trust and embrace my feelings.
- » Unconditional joy is my birthright.
- » I am a divine sexual being.
- » I give and receive love freely.

EMPLOYING YOUR PERSONAL MANTRAS WITH THE SCIENCE OF REPETITION

Now that you have an idea of how to create your personal mantras, how do you use them? This is where the science of personal mantras comes in.

Our minds are in the habit of thinking in particular ways—oftentimes ways that don't support our highest interests. Our thought patterns are formed by our life experiences and influenced by our families of origin, peers, culture, and the society in which we live. Every thought you think strengthens the circuitry in your brain known as neural pathways, and a singular thought either reinforces an existing neural pathway or can produce a new one.

Think of a neural pathway as a groove in the road. When the groove is truly deep, it's hard to get the car out of it if you get stuck. But once you do, you can start down a new path—and then the magic happens. The old, now unused path begins to disappear. Modern brain science has proved that our brains are malleable and have neural plasticity, and that we have the ability, at any age, to rewire our brains. We can use mantras to form new neural pathways; with repetition, the old, formerly dominant pathways diminish and new thought patterns take hold.

To create a practice with your mantras, it is therefore important to cultivate the habit of mantra repetition. Here are some suggested ways to get the most out of them:

» Write your mantras on sticky notes and place them around your house, in your car, at your office, or wherever you'll see them regularly.

» In the morning, when you're getting ready for your day, take a minute to say them out loud to yourself in the mirror.

» Choose one mantra to meditate on for five minutes every morning.

» Journal your mantras, writing them out over a page or two.

PRACTICE

DRAWING ON TRADITION BY CHANTING *VAM*

One of the simplest classical second chakra mantras involves chanting *Vam* (pronounced "vum").

Vam is the traditional Sanskrit mantra known as a bija (seed sound) of the sacral chakra. When you chant *Vam*, the frequency of the sound vibration is believed to cleanse this chakra, bringing healing, balance, and harmony.

To begin this practice, find a comfortable seated position with your lower back supported and your spine straight. Put your phone on "do not disturb" and consider setting a timer for five minutes. I like the Insight Timer meditation app because it has a chime that rings instead of an alarm, which can be jarring at the end of meditating. See https://insighttimer.com.

Close your eyes. Take a few moments to become present by simply breathing deeply through your nose. As you inhale, fill your lungs while expanding your belly. You might even want to put your hands on your abdominal area to feel it expand. On the exhale, breathe out all the air. Let your hands sense the decrease in pressure. Continue this mindful breathing for a few rounds.

As you breathe, focus your attention on the area where your sacral chakra resides, imagining a warm orange glow radiating from within. When you feel centered, take a deep breath through your nose, and on the next exhalation, open your mouth and softly chant *Vam*. Let your tongue rest gently behind your lower teeth, and generate the sound from the back of your throat. You will feel a vibration in your neck and chest.

When your timer goes off, take a few moments to notice how you feel. Wiggle your fingers, stretch, open your eyes, and proceed with your day.

SUMMARY

You can choose to work with your sacral chakra by making your own empowering mantras or repeating the traditional *Vam* bija seed. Either way, the key to your sacral chakra lies in mantra repetition. As with everything in life, practice improves performance. Explore what feels right for you, and give yourself permission to try something new. You never know what miracles await you.

12

COLORS AND SHAPES

GINA NICOLE

There are many fabulous natural ways to activate and attune your sacral chakra so you can enjoy an optimal life. My two favorite methods are using shapes and full-spectrum colors, and this chapter will show you how to use these methods to attune your sacral chakra.

MY SECOND CHAKRA STORY

The second chakra is an especially important chakra for health because of its far-reaching impact. I should know. During my last two years of college, I hit rock bottom. My grandmother—my favorite person in the world—died. I underwent a heartbreaking split from a boyfriend. My sacral chakra, the center of emotions, felt completely void.

In attempting to fix my feelings, I became a fanatic for success. I overdid improving my health, becoming addicted to diet pills. While working on my master's degree, I over-committed to the point where I finished a two-year pro-gram in a single year. But those behaviors didn't address my internal pain and deep sense of deprivation. I developed a full-blown eating disorder.

As synchronicity would have it, I was introduced to Reiki, an energy medicine practice. During my first session, I felt normal! At the end of the session, the practitioner said, "Your second chakra is out of balance."

Eventually, I took up feng shui, which employs the place-ment of objects in a space, as well as color and shape, to create positive energy. As I slowly healed my second chakra and the deep-seated emotional issues lying within it, I learned how to manage my disordered eating and activate the energy in my sacral chakra to enjoy feeling satiated both physically and in my soul.

You don't have to master healing arts to apply these con-cepts to your sacral self. You've only to listen to your body and heed the wisdom of the second chakra—and use cre-ativity as an asset to do so.

WORKING WITH SHAPES

Although there are many shapes you can use for strong acti-vation, the following seven shapes are most helpful for sup-porting the second chakra.

Circle

BENEFITS: Circles are traditionally associated with the second chakra. They form boundaries that provide safety and supportive energy. They help you trust your intuition so you can move forward securely.

VISUALLY: Picture an egg around you. The rounded walls enable the nourishment needed for creativity. You can imagine them around any person, place, or thing to increase their trustworthiness. Circles are connected to the metal element, which activates protection, efficiency, focus, and the health of the second chakra.

QUALITIES WHEN OVERUSED: Too armored, not trusting.

Cross

BENEFITS: The cross is a basic universal shape associated with the sacral chakra in that it symbolizes relationships. The cross brings in energy that invites intimacy. It will promote intuitive and connected moments to help you process deep emotions brought up in your connections with others.

VISUALLY: Picture the cross in your mind and focus on a desire through the center junction.

QUALITIES WHEN OVERUSED: Suffering from painful emotions.

Icosahedron

BENEFITS: This unique shape invites transformation and fluidity.

VISUALLY: A twenty-faced shape, the icosahedron connects us to the element of water and is the fifth and final platonic solid. See it as a container for energy; ask for help and allow universal wisdom to enter through its walls. You don't have to do things alone.

QUALITIES WHEN OVERUSED: Overdoing, not fully transforming.

Lotus

BENEFITS: The six-petaled lotus can represent anger, jealousy, cruelty, hatred, pride, and desire, six emotional states to overcome and purify for connection to the Divine, collective unity, and the abundance that blossoms from these.

VISUALLY: I like to envision the lotus flower rising through the mud and blossoming into a beautiful purified state. When the petals of a lotus point outward, it is symbolic of the opening of our wisdom.

QUALITIES WHEN OVERUSED: Disconnected, bypassing, staying stuck.

Moon Crescent

BENEFITS: The moon crescent is commonly associated with the sacral chakra. It represents fertility, luck, new beginnings, and the connection between the moon and the water—hence our term "moon-water chakra." The phases of the moon have long been known to affect the outcome of the tides and promote a balanced, ebb-and-flow approach to living.

VISUALLY: A moon crescent looks like an eye, reminding you that you are intuitively guided to live the dream you wish for and become fulfilled.

QUALITIES WHEN OVERUSED: Too many changes, overly emotional.

Spiral

BENEFITS: It can be challenging to be creative when you hang on to old emotions and stories. The spiral represents letting go, releasing, and growth.

VISUALLY: Imagine a spiral moving outward from your second chakra to clear the energy blocking new births. Symbolizing connectivity to the Divine, the spiral journeys from your outer ego into your intuitive inner soul.

QUALITIES WHEN OVERUSED: Having a difficult time making space for play, control issues.

Wavy Shapes

BENEFITS: Wavy shapes represent water energy, which is supportive of the second chakra. Such forms are associated with emotions, fluidity, staying in the flow of creativity, cleansing, and purification.

VISUALLY: Access any wavy shape to clear and cleanse your sacral chakra.

QUALITIES WHEN OVERUSED: Being oversensitive to others' feelings, taking on others' energy.

ACTIVATE WATER
USING A SHAPE

It is vital to stay hydrated when working with sacral energy. You can activate your drinking water by using a water bottle or glass with a shape on it.

Trace a shape on your bottle or glass with your little finger (the finger associated with the second chakra) or use stickers to attune to flow and aliveness. When you fill your bottle or glass, feel, sense, or visualize the outcome of a desire in your mind's eye. Simultaneously assert an affirmation in present tense to actualize the intention, such as:

I am purification.

I feel alive in my being.

You can explore different shapes and intentions, changing the affirmation above to fit your desire. For instance, employ a circle for boundaries or a spiral for intimacy or money.

USING A CIRCLE
TO RELEASE TENSION

As the circle is traditionally associated with the second chakra, you can use the shape to activate your sacral energy, releasing whatever is stuck within. One way I do this is to use my body to make hip circles. As I learned in my feng shui training, energy naturally moves from left to right, so I make circles in that direction.

Employ an affirmation such as this one:

> *I am full of life. I feel creation in the*
> *sensual pleasures that life delivers.*

Know that you can interact with shapes in any way that feels right. Play with the symbolism and try different combinations to see their benefits.

WORKING WITH COLOR

I love attuning the water-moon chakra with color. The second chakra is linked with the color orange, which aids you in becoming more confident, enhances your creativity, encourages you to enjoy life's sensual pleasures, and supports other subtle energies within your second chakra.

How do you employ orange to enhance your second chakra? Here are some brief and simple ideas:

» Think in orange. Pretend all thoughts are emerging from your head in an orange hue.

» Wear orange. If you can't get by with an orange suit or dress, go with orange undergarments.

» Draw with orange. Doodle on your notes or make your daily task list using orange pens.

» Carry orange stones. Carnelian, anyone?

» Focus the hue on your navel. Flood the sacral chakra with orange, imagining it entering and moving downward from your belly button. You can also put a hand there and send that orange energy through it.

» Put orange in the environment. This cheery color in a carpet, pillow, candle, or any other object will open your second chakra to its passions.

» Eat orange foods. There is a long list of luscious orange ingredients beyond the obvious oranges and carrots. See the final chapter's recipes.

» You can also play outside the box and employ the full color spectrum. Color is energy and energy is color, and your sacral chakra interacts with all the other in-body chakras. The oneness of our human collective has proved that every subtle energy particle exists in everything else.

EIGHT COLORS FOR
ENLIGHTENING YOUR SACRAL CHAKRA

I use eight colors for second chakra activation, and only one is orange! As you examine each color, pay attention to the various representations, meanings, and support it provides. I have also shared suggestions on how you can use a particular color to activate and attune your sacral chakra. The ideas in the previous section work with all colors.

Red

> **BENEFITS**: Red activates the energies needed for a healthy sacral chakra. It enhances feelings of safety, enhances intuition, sparks innovation, and supports sensuality and intimacy. This fiery color also aids in killing microbes.
>
> **QUALITIES WHEN OVERUSED**: Aggravates intense emotion, increases inflammation.
>
> **SAMPLE AFFIRMATION**: *I see my passion spread with this energetic red.*

Pink

> **BENEFITS**: Pink encourages sacral chakra sensations of love and helps you ground your ability to manifest in the earthly world. Pink is a combination of red (fire) and white (spiritual) energy and will grow your intuitive powers.

QUALITIES WHEN OVERUSED: Lack of self-confidence and trust in self.

SAMPLE AFFIRMATION: *Pink is actualizing what I think.* (Be sure to use this statement only when in a positive mental state.)

Orange

BENEFITS: Orange boosts the entire second chakra, balancing emotions, promoting empathy, and enriching creativity. Go orange when you need more confidence and trust. It is literally a mix of red (fire and passion) and yellow (joy and esteem) and encourages fun and empowerment.

QUALITIES WHEN OVERUSED: Stirs up emotions and hypersensitivities, untrustworthiness.

SAMPLE AFFIRMATION: *Orange boosts my empathy and encourages healthy intimacy.*

Yellow

BENEFITS: A color of structure and self-esteem, yellow enables your sacral chakra to embody personal power and joy. It will balance any worries within this chakra.

QUALITIES WHEN OVERUSED: Feeds fear, control issues, and digestive issues.

SAMPLE AFFIRMATION: *The color yellow transmutes my worrisome emotions so I can move forward with empowering thoughts.*

Green

BENEFITS: This very calming color promotes healing and self-care. Regarding the second chakra, green will assist with healing intimacy and sexuality challenges, balancing discord between the sex organs, kidneys, and lumbar spine.

QUALITIES WHEN OVERUSED: Overly cautious, forced growth.

SAMPLE AFFIRMATION: *This green is healing all discord.*

Blue

BENEFITS: Though blue is not commonly linked to the sacral chakra, it's beneficial to imagine blue there when it's hard to trust what you want to share, especially in conversation with challenging people. Blue is a calming color and will bring you peace in your messaging.

QUALITIES WHEN OVERUSED: Oversharing, trusting the wrong people with a message.

SAMPLE AFFIRMATION: *I calmly and intimately connect with you through the soothing color blue.*

Violet/Purple

BENEFITS: Purple is formed by combining blue (communication and sharing) and red (power and grounding). It is an illuminating color. When used at the second chakra, it activates your intuitive gifts and helps you bring through visions for the future.

QUALITIES WHEN OVERUSED:

Overplanning, frenzied creating.

SAMPLE AFFIRMATION: *I see and feel my optimal life flow illuminated in a purple glow.*

Black

BENEFITS: Black appears in the energy field or chakras where there is discord or discontent. It can also absorb disease or what is not working. Use it to absorb the emotional debris negatively impacting you in the sacral chakra.

QUALITIES WHEN OVERUSED:

Concealing, too much shadow.

SAMPLE AFFIRMATION: *As all emotional discord is absorbed with black, I feel connected and creative.*

NOTE: When removing or absorbing energy, always fill in the empty space with bright light.

SUMMARY

The world is made of color and shape. Your sacral chakra—your home of emotions, feelings, and innovation—responds beautifully to a variety of colors and several different shapes. Use your imagination, intuition, or decor (in clothing or home environment) to bliss out that sacral chakra.

13

RECIPES

It's time for truly delectable joy. Here you'll be treated to amazing recipes customized for your sacral chakra.

Who doesn't love to eat? Cooking with ingredients specific to a chakra is in vogue all over the world. Every chakra is best supported and can most suitably thrive if fed the substances that match its unique set of frequencies. After all, foods have frequencies—and so do chakras. Pair them up and you are good to go.

This chapter features recipes by two wellness experts.

Part 1 provides recipes by longtime health and wellness advocate Anthony J. W. Benson. He has enjoyed a plant-based diet for over thirty-five years, published vegan cookbooks, and loves developing delicious and healthy new recipes. You do not have to be a vegan or vegetarian to enjoy his creations, just a fan of delectable food. Just so you know the differences, veganism is the practice of eating food that isn't derived from animal products, including butter, milk, or eggs. Vegetarianism is similar; it embraces a diet mainly focused on grains, nuts, fruits, and vegetables but can also include dairy and eggs. If you eat seafood, poultry, or meat, you'll still enjoy his plant-based recipes, which are chock-full of healthy ingredients sure to bolster your water-moon chakra.

Part 2 offers tasty recipes from chef and author Susan Weis-Bohlen, whose cuisine features the ancient Indian Ayurvedic system of cookery, which approaches eating from the perspective of balance. Ayurvedic recipes often include dairy and milk products and can be supplemented with seafood, poultry, and meat.

Get ready to nourish your sacral chakra and your entire body.

PART 1

ANTHONY J. W. BENSON

The sacral chakra is associated with the element of water and the color orange. It governs creativity, emotions, joy, enthusiasm, and sensuality. It is also believed to be responsible for the power we feel and ultimately share with the world.

I connect with this notion because creativity and joy are core to my being—and probably yours too. Through my own growth and educational process, I have learned to better respect the influence and impact of color, food, and more on my subtle body and energy centers. It makes sense to support your sacral chakra and energy with healthy, nurturing orange foods—the core approach to eating for this chakra.

CHOOSING ORANGE

I don't know about you, but I have always been drawn to and delighted by orange foods. Who doesn't enjoy a succulent ripe peach on a hot summer day or a delicious piece of pumpkin pie during the holidays (or anytime, for that matter)?

Let's dig a little deeper.

What is the actual connection between us and food? Simply put, the energetic vibration of food interacts with our own inherent vibration. The result? We experience energy reciprocity. The mutual vibrational exchange nurtures our chakras; thus, our chakras get activated and energized. Therefore, eating mindful, healthy foods equates to healthy chakras. In this case, orange is where it's at for supporting the second chakra. For example, papayas, peaches, melons, mangoes, and other sweet orange fruits are good healing food for the sacral chakra. The spice cinnamon is also helpful, as is drinking lots of water.

Many of us have definite and emotional opinions about what and how to eat. As someone who ate poorly when younger and has eaten a plant-based diet for more than half my life, I sure do. Conscious choices about what we eat are an integral part of healthy living. So, what is the "right way" to eat? I maintain that it's the best way for *you* and your overall health. The key is discovering what best serves your body, mind, and spirit. If supporting your chakras is what you seek, then eating correlating food colors for each energy center is always helpful, regardless of your chosen dietary direction. Thus, if your second chakra needs a boost, chow down on orange foods!

Here is a partial list of some of the foods that balance the sacral chakra and are predominately orange:

» carrot

» butternut squash

» mango

» orange

» peach

» apricot

» sweet potato

» pumpkin

» orange bell pepper

» papaya

Orange-colored foods are often high in specific carotenoids that are an excellent way to balance and open the sacral chakra.

To best balance and support your sacral chakra, it is also essential to stay hydrated, so drink plenty of water throughout the day. In addition, you might consider infusing your water with fresh orange or mango for added flavor enhancement as well as energetic benefits.

These orange-based meals and consistent hydration will help you maintain an energetic sacral balance.

Diversify your home menu options and energize your sacral chakra with these three delectable plant-based second chakra recipes. There is one each for breakfast, lunch, and dinner. I recommend choosing organic food whenever possible.

Peach, Mango, and Orange Sacral Smoothie

SERVES 1

Shift your creativity and love of life with this delicious smoothie.

1 mango
1 peach
1 orange
½ cup any plant-based milk of choice
½ cup ice cubes
1 tablespoon maple syrup (optional and to taste)

If using frozen fruit, reduce or eliminate ice cubes based on the desired consistency.

Peel, chop, and place peach, mango, and orange in a blender. Add plant-based milk of choice and ice cubes. Add maple syrup or another natural sweetener, if desired, to taste. Blend until smooth and serve cold.

Creativity Carrot Salad

SERVES 2

I recommend letting the dish sit for an hour or so in the refrigerator to blend the flavors—if you can wait that long!

- 1 pound carrots, washed, peeled, and trimmed
- ¼ cup extra virgin olive oil or avocado oil
- 1 crushed garlic clove
- 2–3 tablespoons fresh lemon juice (about half a lemon) or bottled lemon juice
- 1 teaspoon Dijon mustard
- 2 tablespoons maple syrup
- ½ teaspoon harissa (adjust to taste)
- 2 tablespoons finely chopped fresh mint
- ¼ teaspoon ground cinnamon
- ⅛ teaspoon paprika
- ⅛ teaspoon ground cumin
- ½ teaspoon sea salt
- Freshly ground black pepper to taste
- ⅓ cup toasted pine nuts
- ½ cup Sultana raisins or finely chopped dates
- 1 cup chopped curly parsley

Grate or shred the carrots. In a large bowl, whisk to combine the oil, garlic, lemon juice, mustard, maple syrup, harissa, mint, cinnamon, paprika, and cumin. Add salt and pepper. Add the shredded carrots, pine nuts, raisins or dates, and parsley. Toss well to coat.

Sweet Potato Pumpkin Stew

SERVES 2

This hearty stew will fill you up for hours.

    1 tablespoon avocado oil
    1 medium onion, chopped
    2 large sweet potatoes, peeled and cubed
    1 cup canned pumpkin puree
    2 carrots, peeled and sliced
    1 orange bell pepper, chopped
    2 cloves garlic, minced
    1 cup chopped celery
    1 15-ounce can diced tomatoes
    1 cup low-sodium vegetable stock
    1 tablespoon soy sauce or tamari
    1 bay leaf
    Sea salt and ground pepper to taste

Heat a large saucepan over medium-high heat. Add avocado oil and onion and cook for 3 to 5 minutes until translucent. Add the rest of the ingredients, reduce heat to low, and simmer for 30 to 40 minutes, adding more stock as needed. Serve hot as-is or with a grain of choice, if desired.

If you're seeking extra healing power for your sacral chakra, add spices like turmeric, ginger, or cumin to this dish for added impact. Feel free to adapt these recipes as your creativity and palate dictate. I encourage you to explore and discover other dishes that help you attune to your body, chakras, and overall health and well-being.

PART 2

SUSAN WEIS-BOHLEN

The sacral chakra resides in the tender area between the first and third chakras, in the lower abdomen. This is not an area I was on good terms with when I was younger. I often had stomach aches and pains. I was told to suck in my tummy or hide it behind large T-shirts or a towel at the pool. When I learned about the qualities of the second chakra, I heaved a sigh of relief and allowed my belly to go soft. By gripping and holding tightly onto this area of the body, I was causing discomfort, restricting my creativity, disconnecting from my sexuality, and depriving myself of connecting on a deeper level to myself and others.

By letting go, I was able to feel into this sacred space in a way I hadn't before. I began to do "belly meditations," rubbing the sacral chakra region in a clockwise motion with an open palm, sending loving-kindness and acceptance to myself, tapping into a watery sense of movement, inspiration, and possibilities. I learned that ancient Vedic words associated with this chakra are *purity, nourishment, charm,* and *merging.*

We can feed the sacral chakra with these notions in mind, as well as the elemental qualities of this area. Moving from the first chakra (earth element) into the second chakra (water element), the color shifts from red to orange. By eating food that supports these elemental signifiers, we can nourish ourselves on a deeper level.

The recipes I'm providing are based on the ancient science of Ayurveda, which assures balance among ingredients. Because they are devoted to the sacral chakra, orange plays a prominent role, as does food from the ocean, such as seafood, seaweed, and sea salt. A bit of earthiness comes into play to keep the sacral chakra functioning in conjunction with the root chakra, as they all work best when activated in an equalizing manner.

As we say in Ayurveda, food is medicine. Stay hydrated. Eat orange foods. You can wear orange clothes too! Cook with a sense of playfulness and happiness: dance around the kitchen, and eat only when you are in a good mood, free from distractions. Enjoy every bite of these anytime recipes.

"Morning After" Drink

SERVES 2

Strenuous exercise and sexual activity can deplete the essence of life that flows through you. This energy of life is called the *ojas* in Sanskrit. You can replenish your ojas with this rich, vitality-boosting drink. This is not an everyday concoction, but rather one to enjoy with your lover, or on your own after a night (or day) of overextension that may leave you feeling depleted.

> ½ cup raw, unsalted almonds, skins removed (soak overnight or blanch in hot water and the skins will slide off)
>
> 2 cups dairy or plant-based milk
>
> 3 large dried dates, chopped
>
> ¼ teaspoon powdered cardamom
>
> ¼ teaspoon powdered ginger
>
> ¼ teaspoon powdered cinnamon
>
> Pinch of sea salt
>
> One strand saffron (optional)

Mix all ingredients in a blender until smooth. You can add more milk if needed. Drink at room temperature or heat on the stove in a small saucepan. Sip slowly, and feel the drink rejuvenating your tissues, blood, bone, and brain.

Sacral Chakra Juice

SERVES I

You can use a juicer or blender for this recipe. A juicer will remove the fiber to give a blast of energy. A blender leaves the fiber in, which makes the nutrients tougher to extract but helps counterbalance the sweetness. Drink the juice on an empty stomach, and eat solid food only when you feel hungry.

> 2 whole oranges, rinsed, with the peel on
> (creates a satisfying bitter flavor)
> 3 carrots
> 1 whole mango, pit removed
> 1 cup blueberries

Add all ingredients one by one to the juicer.

If using a blender, chop the ingredients and add everything together with 1 cup water. Blend on high until relatively smooth. Drink immediately.

Roasted Sweet Potatoes with Oranges

SERVES 4

This naturally sweet and vibrant dish will spark creativity and desire and satisfy you on every level. Roasting sweet potatoes glazed in orange zest and juice with spices will fill your senses with aroma and color and surprise your taste buds. Serve over wilted greens or a bowl of quinoa for a complete meal or use as a side dish with a second chakra protein like orange roughy, salmon, shrimp, or any fowl or meat dish.

> 4 large sweet potatoes (peeled or unpeeled, your choice)
> 2 tablespoons olive or avocado oil
> Zest and juice of 1 large orange
> 1 teaspoon cinnamon powder
> 1 teaspoon sea salt (or to taste)
> 1 teaspoon rosemary powder
> Black pepper to taste

Preheat the oven to 450°F and lightly oil a large baking sheet. Cut the sweet potatoes into cubes approximately the same size and place in a bowl. Add the oil, orange zest and juice, and spices, and stir to coat the potatoes well.

Pour the mixture onto the baking sheet and spread it out into one layer (use two sheets if you need more room). Roast for about 20 minutes, remove and stir to avoid burning, and cook 15 minutes more or until potatoes are browned.

Orange Roughy with Gomasio

SERVES 4

Orange roughy is an extraordinary fish; it can live for more than two hundred years. It's red when in the sea but turns orange once caught. The texture after cooking is flaky, and the taste is mild and sweet. With the addition of the low-sodium Japanese sea salt/sesame seed blend called gomasio, this recipe creates the perfect second chakra food. Look for gomasio with seaweed added.

> 2 tablespoons lemon juice
> 1 tablespoon melted ghee or butter
> ½ teaspoon dried thyme
> ½ teaspoon lemon zest
> ½ teaspoon black pepper
> 1 teaspoon gomasio with seaweed
> 4 orange roughy fillets, about 6 ounces each

Mix the lemon juice, ghee or butter, and spices in a bowl. Dip the fish into the bowl and cover completely on both sides. Transfer the fish to a well-oiled sheet pan and place under the oven broiler for about 4 minutes on each side. Once the fish is flaky, it's done, so watch closely because broiler heat varies.

Alternatively, place the fillets in a well-oiled skillet and cook over medium heat on the stovetop. Cover and allow the fillets to cook through for about 10 minutes.

SUMMARY

Between Anthony and Susan's recipes, you have a full day of recipes and healthy snack foods galore. Your sacral chakra will love being nurtured with celebratory orange foods and foods high in mineral and water content. Love your second chakra, and it will love you back!

CONCLUSION

Think how hard it would be to appreciate the world—or yourself—without the many-petaled functions of your second chakra. Though we often say that the eyes are the doorway to the soul, the truth is that your sacral chakra is the true portal to the soul and everything beautiful, internal and external.

In this book, I have sometimes called this subtle energy center your "water-moon" chakra. Like water, it enables the flow of intuition, emotions, and creativity. Like the moon, it reflects truth, calling you to reflect your being into the universe. Named *svadhisthana* in Sanskrit, this chakra enables the sacred practice of flowering into your life.

Within the pages of part 1, you parted the veils of time to delve into the ancients' understandings of this sensuous center. Revealed as various shades of orange, the hues and tones of this chakra express frequencies that bring about manifestation, often a result of owning and sharing emotions. Centered within the bodily geography of the sacral vertebrae and abdomen, this center physically pulses with the electrical and chemical components of feelings, also determining much of your reproductive, immune, and gastrointestinal health.

Throughout part 2, you enjoyed chakra experts who helped you dive into various pools of second chakra knowledge. You gained tools for continually guiding yourself into a healthy, supportive relationship with your second chakra by drawing upon spirit allies, yoga exercises, body awareness activities, meditations, vibrational remedies, sound techniques, cooking experiences, and so much more.

By this time, my hope is that you've emerged as your own totally second chakra self. Whether you'd describe that self using terms like *practical*, *bohemian*, *lucid*, or *dreamlike*, your sacral chakra is *you*.

ANTHONY J. W. BENSON serves as a creative business strategist, manager, coach, producer, and writer specializing in working with consciously awake authors, speakers, musicians, entrepreneurs, and small and large businesses. He has shared his expertise on numerous podcasts and radio and television shows. Anthony has led a mindful plant-based lifestyle for over 35 years.

ANTHONYJWBENSON.COM
INJOICREATIVE.COM

NITIN BHATNAGAR, DO, is an intuitive cardiologist, life architect, metaphysician, energy medicine healer, human behavioral specialist, and international inspirational speaker. He completed his medical school and post-graduate training in internal medicine and cardiology and has authored articles for many outlets. He has also studied alternative healing modalities, including Reiki and color medicine, and is a CrossFit and nutrition coach and endurance athlete.

WHEELSOFTHEMIND.COM

© Atikin Photographics

JO-ANNE BROWN is an intuitive, energy healer, and author who lives in central Queensland, Australia, with a background including engineering and bioresonance therapy. She helps highly sensitive people find meaning in their profound emotional experiences and release disharmonious patterns. She is featured in the internationally best-selling multi-author book *Intuitive: Speaking Her Truth*.

JOANNEINTUITIVE.COM

© Michelle Francesconi

AMANDA HUGGINS is an anxiety and mindfulness coach, certified yoga instructor, podcast host, author, and speaker. Her signature "Scientific, Spiritual, Practical" approach has helped thousands achieve transformation in mind, body, and soul. Besides presenting online courses, Amanda offers guidance on her podcast, *Anxiety Talks with Amanda*, and has an online community of over a half million followers.

INSTAGRAM AND TIKTOK @ITSAMANDAHUGGINS
AMANDAHUGGINSCOACHING.COM

© Forever Studios

MARGARET ANN LEMBO is the author of *The Essential Guide to Crystals, Chakra Awakening, Animal Totems and the Gemstone Kingdom, The Essential Guide to Aromatherapy and Vibrational Healing, Angels and Gemstone Guardians Cards, Gemstone Guardians and Your Soul Purpose,* among other titles. She is an award-winning aromatherapist and the owner of The Crystal Garden, the conscious living store and center of the Palm Beaches.

MARGARETANNLEMBO.COM
THECRYSTALGARDEN.COM

© Ashley Carrington Photography

GINA NICOLE is a feng shui consultant, subtle energy medicine practitioner, and the author of a deck of wisdom cards. She encourages empathic people to orient their minds, bodies, spirits, and homes to align with higher frequencies to make impeccably clear and intuitive decisions. She loves to travel and is devoted to bringing transformational light to the foster care system.

GINANICOLE.NET

© Trina Yin

TIA TUENGE is a transformational coach, energy healer, wellness facilitator, yoga instructor, and scholar of ancient feminine history. She has a passion for teaching, mentoring, and hosting sacred gatherings that include women's circles, sound baths, tea ceremonies, retreats, and corporate events. She has been trained as a council facilitator at the prestigious Ojai Foundation and in Reiki, crystal healing, and many versions of yoga.

ARTOFSACREDLIVING.COM

© Daniel Chambo Photography

AMELIA VOGLER is a grounding and energy medicine specialist, internationally respected teacher of energy medicine, spiritual coach, and meditation guide. She embeds essential energetic practices in her meditations and teachings to better humanity. Maintaining an international private practice, she has helped thousands of individuals transform through grounding practices, intuitive insight, and advanced energy medicine.

AMELIAVOGLER.COM
VOGLERINSTITUTE.COM

SUSAN WEIS-BOHLEN is certified in Ayurveda from the Chopra Center and has studied with Dr. Vasant Lad and Amadea Morningstar. She has also served on the National Ayurvedic Medical Association (NAMA) Board of Directors since 2018. A former bookstore owner, Susan is also the author of *Ayurveda Beginner's Guide: Essential Ayurvedic Principles and Practices to Balance and Heal Naturally* and *Seasonal Self-Care Rituals: Eat, Breathe, Move, and Sleep Better— According to Your Dosha.*

BREATHEAYURVEDA.COM